Caligula EMPEROR OF ROME

ARTHER FERRILL

Caligula

EMPEROR OF ROME

with 19 illustrations

THAMES AND HUDSON

To my mother and to the memory of my father

© 1991 Thames and Hudson Ltd, London

First published in the United States in 1991 by
Thames and Hudson Inc., 500 Fifth Avenue,
New York, New York 10110

Library of Congress Catalog Card Number 88-51351

Printed and bound in Yugoslavia

Contents

Preface

One spring day in AD 40 the Roman Emperor Caligula stood with the mighty legions of the Empire and looked out over the English Channel towards Britain. Julius Caesar had twice crossed those turbulent waters almost one hundred years earlier, but since that time no Roman legion had marched on British soil. The conquest of Britain was a great Roman dream, and Caligula, soon to proclaim himself a god, hoped to win the glory of taking for Rome what was thought to be the very edge and end of the world. Not even Alexander the Great, near the eastern limits of civilization, had gone so far.

What happened on the Channel was a sham, a scene so incredible that many modern historians have actually refused to believe it, although the evidence is firm and unshakeable. The Emperor had probably already been hailed as Britannicus, in anticipation of a great victory, but, instead of ordering an assault across the water, Caligula turned back after an abortive embarkation in a command trireme. Then he lined his army up in battle array on the Roman side of the Channel, moved in the catapults and the siege engines, and stunned the entire force by sounding a charge while at the same time ordering his men to pick up seashells. The shells were, according to the Emperor, 'plunder from the sea'. Caligula proclaimed a great victory, and commemorated it by constructing a lighthouse on the coast like Alexander's at Pharos. After paying the troops a victory bonus, he turned about and tried to decimate some of his legions. When the response was anger and mutiny, Caligula abandoned the entire project and rushed back to Rome to celebrate his 'success' formally.

Later Roman historians and biographers considered this one of Caligula's craziest acts. Only a demented ruler could have behaved in such a fashion. Indeed, what had Rome come to? How could the world's mightiest empire, the preserver of man's loftiest civilization, have fallen into the hands of a madman? Later in this book we shall return to this famous episode in the life of the Emperor Caligula. It actually happened, and it does raise fascinating questions about the nature of insanity and political power in an otherwise sane and successfully functional governmental structure. It will not do, as so many modern historians have tried, to deny the historicity of the story. In recent years Idi Amin and the Emperor Bokassa have shown that genuinely crazy men can become heads of state in a generally rational world. The insanity at issue here is not the madness and calculated cruelty of a Hitler, a Stalin or a Tojo. It is purely wild, arbitrary, irrational craziness – sometimes cruel, sometimes humorous, occasionally driven by perverted policy, but usually simply mercurial and capricious.

Few 'mad' rulers are as well known as the Roman Emperor Caligula. Although his achievement was in no way as great as his notoriety, he was an unusually significant emperor, influencing his contemporaries in a manner he never dreamed, setting a tone by example for serious, philosophical discussions of the good monarch versus the tyrant.[1] Resolute in will and dissolute in life, Caligula sometimes entertained and often terrified the people around him. Like most villains in history, he was not all bad, and the famous Roman biographer Suetonius, in the *Lives of the Twelve Caesars*, credited the Emperor with some virtuous acts. After dealing with those few virtues, however, Suetonius said, 'So much for the prince, now for the monster', a statement which is often quoted.[2] Needless to say, Caligula the monster required about twice as much space as Caligula the prince.

In the twentieth century Caligula has received much attention in the works of scholars, novelists, playwrights, and in movies and television. The Caligula of the popular media has been mainly the monster, the mad Emperor who planned to make his horse a consul of the Roman people. The Caligula of classical scholarship, on the other hand, has been a maligned prince, a rational, sometimes shrewd manipulator in a hostile world of jealous, disgruntled senatorial aristocrats and in a scheming, ruthless family, riddled with dynastic ambition. According to this view, Caligula, victimized by his contemporaries, was also traduced by his biographer, the scandal-monger Suetonius, and by a later Roman historian, Dio Cassius, who wrote in Greek.[3] Their works are the major surviving sources for the life and reign of Caligula, and classical scholars are justly cautious in accepting as historical fact the rumours and innuendo of those biased and often careless authors.[4]

Nevertheless, the Emperor Caligula was a fascinating creature in his own day and has continued in modern times to intrigue a wide audience. As the stereotypically crazy ruler, he appeared in the popular novel and movie, *The Robe*, in Robert Graves' *I, Claudius* (dramatized for television by the BBC), and even in an x-rated, sexually explicit film, produced by the publisher of *Penthouse* magazine. Amazingly, despite the notoriety of his name, there has been no scholarly biography in this century that treats him as a demented tyrant. A book by J.P.V.D. Balsdon, though thoroughly researched and skilfully argued, was essentially a whitewash. Balsdon even refused to call the Emperor by his widely known nickname[5] and entitled his 1934 book *The Emperor Gaius (Caligula)*. Yet we know that the Emperor himself disliked the name Gaius. Anthony Barrett, in his recent biography *Caligula: The Corruption of Power* (1989), does not go as far as Balsdon did in rationalizing the ruler's actions, but Barrett believes that Caligula was not insane and that he was intelligent: 'Caligula was clearly capable of acting right to the end in a rational manner.'[6]

Ironically Balsdon's book appeared in the same year as Robert Graves' novel and both books have had a strong influence. Balsdon's work has been highly praised by professional classicists and ancient historians: it has reigned supreme in university classrooms. Barrett's book will probably now supersede it. On the other hand, Graves' view of a much more diabolical Caligula has attracted a large and enthusiastic following. In this study I hope to demonstrate that the real Caligula, despite much modern scholarship, was in fact a monster and that academic efforts to revise this estimate of him are misguided.

The catalogue of Caligula's vices makes captivating reading, mainly because as ruler of one of the world's most powerful empires, he had the ability to act out all his depraved and violent fantasies, provided he was shameless enough to do so. Modesty and restraint were not among Caligula's many attributes, as even his modern defenders concede. When passion prevailed with Caligula – and, according to Suetonius and Dio Cassius, two of the main ancient sources for the reign, it often did – the Emperor simply yielded to it, apparently without moral qualms or concern for his reputation. Both Suetonius and Dio Cassius say that at dinner parties in the palace he merely helped himself to the wives of his illustrious guests, taking them, usually one at a time, into another room for dalliance (perhaps his only concession to shame) and returning dishevelled to discuss their sexual performance with his friends, including the affected husbands.[7] There is a twisted version of a famous statement, made by Lord Acton, that seems to apply especially well to Caligula: 'Power corrupts, and absolute power is even nicer.'[8]

Modern historians have observed that the conspirators whom Caligula punished so severely were probably actually guilty of plotting to overthrow him. That is indeed likely; but the Machiavellian justification that a prince may strike at anyone who aims at him misses a fundamental point. The real question is whether there was a legitimate reason (as opposed to a personal grudge) for the conspiracies. As we shall see, the most serious conspiracy against Caligula was not motivated by bitter personal differences.

Naturally not everyone in the Roman Empire suffered equally under Caligula. As is often the case under a tyrant, those who were closest to him felt the force of his tyranny, while provincials escaped its worst effects (except, in the case of Caligula, the

Jews). It was in Rome and not in the provinces, in the Senate and not in the streets, that Caligula revealed the monster. The monster was, however, no less real for that fact. Occasionally, as we shall see, even the people saw glimpses of that tortured creature that so resembled their prince. As his reign wore on, relations with the *plebs* deteriorated. In exasperation Caligula once exclaimed: 'Would that the Roman people had but one neck!'⁹ By the time the Emperor was murdered, few Romans in the capital were sad to see him go.

The Julio-Claudian Family

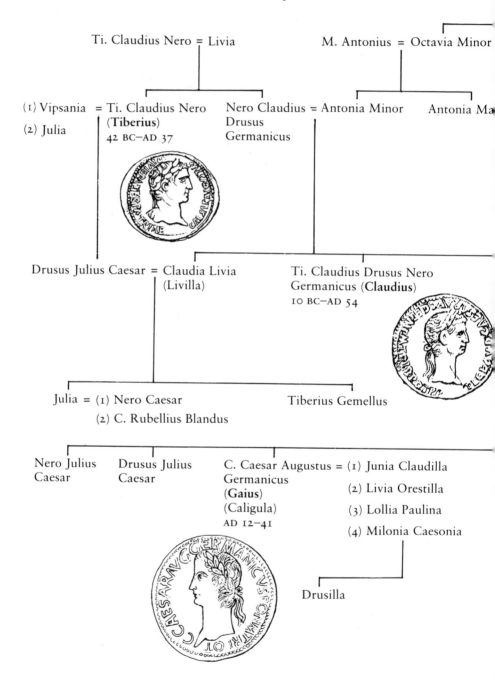

Ti. Claudius Nero = Livia   M. Antonius = Octavia Minor

(1) Vipsania = Ti. Claudius Nero   Nero Claudius = Antonia Minor   Antonia Ma
(2) Julia   **(Tiberius)**   Drusus
          42 BC–AD 37   Germanicus

Drusus Julius Caesar = Claudia Livia   Ti. Claudius Drusus Nero
            (Livilla)   Germanicus (**Claudius**)
                               10 BC–AD 54

Julia = (1) Nero Caesar   Tiberius Gemellus
       (2) C. Rubellius Blandus

Nero Julius   Drusus Julius   C. Caesar Augustus = (1) Junia Claudilla
Caesar   Caesar   Germanicus
                           (**Gaius**)   (2) Livia Orestilla
                           (Caligula)   (3) Lollia Paulina
                           AD 12–41   (4) Milonia Caesonia

Drusilla

Not all family connections are indicated

C. Octavius = Atia

C. Octavius = (1) Scribonia
(**Augustus**)   (2) Livia
63 BC–AD 14

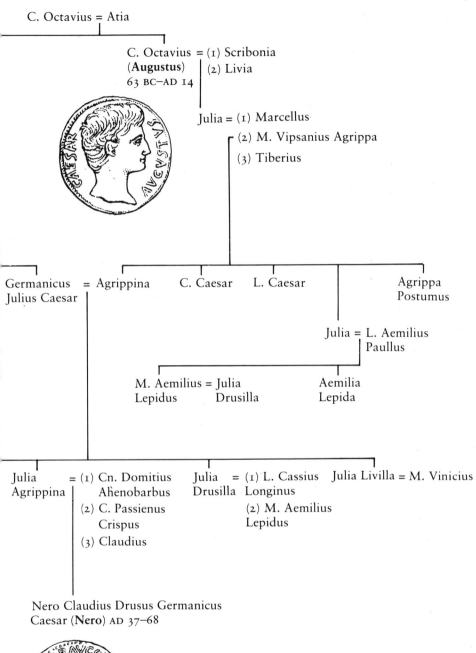

Julia = (1) Marcellus
(2) M. Vipsanius Agrippa
(3) Tiberius

Germanicus = Agrippina   C. Caesar   L. Caesar   Agrippa
Julius Caesar   Postumus

Julia = L. Aemilius
Paullus

M. Aemilius = Julia   Aemilia
Lepidus   Drusilla   Lepida

Julia   = (1) Cn. Domitius   Julia   = (1) L. Cassius   Julia Livilla = M. Vinicius
Agrippina | Ahenobarbus   Drusilla   Longinus
          | (2) C. Passienus   (2) M. Aemilius
          | Crispus   Lepidus
          | (3) Claudius

Nero Claudius Drusus Germanicus
Caesar (**Nero**) AD 37–68

1. The World of a Prince

Caligula was born on 31 August AD 12 at Antium in Italy, the modern Anzio.[10] The Emperor Augustus, now in his seventies, had only two more years of life, so the ageing ruler never knew that this newborn great-grandson would some day scandalize Rome and brand the line of Julius Caesar with infamy. When Augustus died in 14, the whole world mourned its loss and grieved for the family that had produced in Caesar and Augustus two gods and two of the world's greatest and most powerful leaders.[11] The infant Caesar, named Gaius but soon called Caligula, 'Little Boots', because of the boy's military uniform that he wore, never knew his illustrious Julian ancestors.[12] Eventually, however, he became the ruler of the Roman Empire, the heir to the legacy of the Caesars.

The Roman Empire

The Empire of the Romans embraced the entire civilized world, the *orbis terrarum*, at least as far as the Romans themselves were concerned.[13] The claim was slightly boastful – there were barbarians, mainly Germans, living north of the Roman Empire, but they were untamed savages and did not count. To the east, in ancient Babylonia, along the lower stretches of Mesopotamia, was the heart of the decadent, mysterious world of Parthia, but it too somehow did not count in Roman reckoning, though it should have. Romans knew little about India and a great deal less about China and sub-Saharan Africa. For all practical purposes, then, their claim to 'rule the world in peace and justice', to use the words of their greatest poet, Virgil, was almost true as far as they could know and a great deal more true than the later British claim to 'rule the waves'.[14]

The Roman Empire of the first century AD was a marvel of political and military engineering, a structure so vast and so apparently unwieldy that one modern scholar has called it, ironically, an 'impossibility'.[15] With about 6000 miles of frontiers, stretching from the mouth of the Rhine (Britain, as we have seen, was not added until after the death of Caligula) to the cataracts of the Nile, the emperors ruled over an incredible number of ethnic and cultural units. The Roman Empire was the world's first great 'melting pot' of peoples, providing identity and a sense of belonging to various races and languages from the Euphrates to the Atlantic.

Although the Empire was based on an economy that was rural and agricultural, perhaps the most distinguishing feature of its civilization was its cities. The very word 'civilization', from the Latin *civitas* (city), means 'citified'. We may think of the Empire as a cluster of provinces, but there is a sense in which it was mainly a network of cities, and, for the most part, it was life in the cities that mattered.[16] There were the temples and the government buildings, there lived the priests and the politicians, and in the cities was the wealth – drawn from the countryside – that supported the grandeur of Rome. If Caligula was a child of the camps, as is sometimes said, because he accompanied his father Germanicus to the frontiers, he became a man of the city. Yet some knowledge of the rural nature of large parts of the Empire was required of a good emperor, and one of Caligula's greatest failings was his apparent unfamiliarity with the farm. Imperial princes could not actually be farmers, of course, but they could and should know something about rural life. Pride in the rustic origins of Rome was an important part of being Roman, a fact that Augustus, for example, had known well.

Politically the Early Roman Empire was a delicate structure. Augustus had fashioned the emperorship by telling the Romans a great lie, that he was merely one of a number of properly elected officials, more influential than the others, but still simply 'the first among equals'.[17] As we know in modern times, political slogans are often deceitful, but people tolerate them for many reasons. The Romans were actually grateful to Augustus for his 'happy lie' since it permitted them to enjoy the benefits of monarchy while claiming to possess their ancient liberty (*libertas*).[18] Although Augustus ruthlessly exercised autocratic power, he was careful to respect traditional Roman reverence for republican forms of government. There is a sense in which his respect for Rome's past was sincere and not simply a pretence for partisan political purposes. He was in some ways old-fashioned, and the genuineness of his traditionalism made it easier for him to live his happy lie, playing a role he had written for himself.

Unfortunately his successors found the part difficult. It did require a consummate actor, and neither Tiberius, Augustus' immediate successor, nor Caligula, the third of the emperors, was suited for the performance. Tiberius actually tried but made things worse with bad acting; Caligula made no attempt to mask his power and paraded his absolutism for all to see. In the end Caligula's unbridled tyranny led to many of the problems he had with the Roman Senate.

From the beginning the Emperor of Rome had to balance a number of competing special-interest groups. The *plebs* of the city looked to him as a champion, the provider of bread and circuses.[19] For the most part they cared little about his accumulation of power as long as he delivered the services they expected of the central government. Under Augustus crowds actually gathered in the streets demanding that their leader be given the dictatorship. Whenever there was a famine or some other urgent crisis, one response to the problem was to give the Emperor more power. After all, he was the one who could get things done, and he needed the flexibility to act decisively.[20]

On the other hand, some members of the Roman Senate regarded with jealousy the cult of personality and the accretion of power that enveloped the emperorship. Not all of them cared, of course. Many senatorial families had jumped on the imperial bandwagon, and certain senators were among the most outrageous sycophants. Imperial patronage could make or break a senatorial career, so it was natural for ambitious politicians to be careful how they treated the ruler. And some senators, occasionally quite a few, actually liked and admired the Emperor. This was particularly true in the days of Augustus, who was usually fastidiously respectful of the senatorial aristocracy.[21]

Still, the Senate had once been the seat of power in the Roman state, the arbiter of policy and of preference. Some senators, normally a minority, looked back wistfully to those prestigious days when their ancestors had been an assembly of kings, before the Caesars had taken all power. Aristocratic families, descendants of illustrious lines like the Scipios and the Fabians, regarded the Julian princes with envy and disfavour and resented the nearly servile status of the old clans in the new regime. Under Augustus and Tiberius the deference senators were required to show the Emperor went at least to men who had earned their position through hard work, determination, and some considerable skill. Caligula was the first emperor to have his power handed to him on a silver platter, to have had no training for the throne other than the dissolute life of an imperial prince.[22]

Emperors were also responsible for the welfare of their non-Roman, provincial subjects. Augustus had handled that part of his job quite well, creating a new system of provincial administration that relied upon senators as governors but placed them on salary and kept them, generally, scrupulously honest. Inevitably there were some scoundrels – no government is entirely free from them – but the new imperial system of Augustus was much less corrupt than the earlier republican one.[23] Most tax-farming was eliminated, though the hated publicans still collected customs and other minor dues.[24] Provincial tribute, that greatest source of tax revenues, was put into the hands of governmental agents serving the Emperor, and extortion became far less common than it had been earlier. Augustus' imperial system of provincial administration worked so well that, even under bad emperors, life in the provinces prospered. Tyranny and incompetence normally were felt much more in Rome than elsewhere, although the maladministration of an emperor did sometimes affect the whole Empire. We shall see that the provinces were fortunate that Caligula was killed after a relatively brief reign; the effects of his madness would otherwise have extended to the frontiers.

The physical trappings of the emperorship were impressive, setting the ruler apart from other Roman nobles. Augustus was in some ways an abstemious man, disdaining luxurious displays, but he had created a palace on the Palatine – the word comes from the Latin *palatium*, originally meaning the famous hill overlooking the Forum and the Circus Maximus, but eventually used simply to designate the imperial residence (sometimes in the form *palatia*).[25] The first palace of Augustus, where he had lived as Caesar Octavianus from 36 BC, had once belonged to a famous orator, senator and millionaire by the name of Hortensius. In comparison with later palaces it was tiny, but in Augustus' day it was considered quite a lavish mansion. Through agents he purchased the neighbouring houses, cleared the area, and built a new temple to Apollo, which was completed in 28 BC. A public library was constructed on the palace grounds, and the whole area became a major imperial, civic and religious centre. One corner of it opened up onto the Forum.[26]

By the reign of Caligula the palace had become significantly larger. Tiberius added a huge annexe, the so-called *Domus Tiberiana*, and apparently other members of the imperial family, including Caligula's father Germanicus, had constructed additions to the palace.[27] As time went by, the imperial family gained possession of many choice properties in the city, and the Emperor often spent time in these other places. Caligula inherited gardens on the right bank of the Tiber from his mother Agrippina and occasionally spent time there. The famous gardens of Maecenas, the close friend of Augustus, had been left by will to the Emperor; the emperors were frequently named as beneficiaries in the wills of wealthy Romans. Tiberius inherited the Gardens of Sallust from his adviser, Sallustius Crispus, in AD 20. The fact is that by the time of Caligula, the Emperor might be found at any number of luxurious locations in Rome.[28] Outside of Rome, especially in the Bay of Naples, he owned many country estates.[29]

Other physical signs, in addition to the palace and the imperial gardens, set the emperors apart from mortal men. Augustus had been permitted to place laurel wreaths on the doorposts of his house. He was also awarded a civic crown of oak leaves that he put above the door.[30] These symbols of glory certainly became a part of the imperial palace. Emperors were also distinguished by their entourage, including bodyguards and military escorts.[31] They greeted ambassadors and received petitioners in the palace or at the temple of Apollo in the palace grounds, which were open to the public. Thousands of people sometimes gathered for great festival occasions.

Although these markings of power were impressive, in the days of Augustus, Tiberius, and Caligula some of the most commonly adduced symbols of imperial rule were lacking. Historians often talk about the 'imperial throne' but in fact there was none.[32] Another common expression is 'the struggle for the purple', but in the first century AD purple had not yet become synonymous with the emperorship. Far from being an imperial monopoly, purple was widely used by all classes of society, though only the wealthiest Romans could afford the expensive Tyrian purple made from shellfish. Only in the second century did the purple cloak begin to be definitively associated with the Emperor.[33]

It was in fact the lack of a rigid, fixed concept of emperorship that permitted a wild young man like Caligula to act the way he did, at least for as long as he did. Emperors in his day were still shaping their official image and position. What the limits were no one knew, but they were clearly very wide, because the real power of a Caesar was greater than any Roman had ever seen.

This power rested mainly on the support of the legions. Legionaries were notoriously unconcerned about constitutional forms in the city of Rome, caring far more about regular pay and occasional large bonuses than about liberty. When Augustus died in AD 14, there were twenty-five legions stationed around the frontiers of the Empire. Just a few years earlier, in AD 9, three legions had been lost in the great defeat of the Teutoburg Forest against Arminius and the Germans, a defeat that set the Roman frontier at the Rhine and kept Germany free from Romanization.[34] By the time of Caligula in the late 30s there were still only twenty-five legions, which, together with the non-citizen auxiliary troops, made up an army of some 250,000. In a passage from Tacitus' *Annals* for the year AD 23 we know that two legions were stationed in Egypt, three in Spain, four in Syria, one in Africa, eight on the Rhine, and seven along the Danube.[35] Although the economy of force is remarkable, considering the enormous extent of the Roman Empire, the Emperor nevertheless had at his disposal a massive army, one that had many times demonstrated a brutal effectiveness on the field of battle.[36] Strategically the army provided for the imperial defence; politically it supported the ambitions of the reigning Caesar against whatever foe.

In addition to the frontier army, the Emperor of Rome had near at hand various other forces of a military or a paramilitary nature. Best known and most important was the Praetorian Guard. Commanded by the Praetorian Prefect, the Guard, consisting in the Early Empire (at least by the time of Nero and probably earlier) of about 7000 men, was stationed from AD 23 in a single camp just outside Rome. It became in essence the Emperor's special, crack force.[37] For more immediate purposes there was the Batavian bodyguard, whose specially recruited German warriors were fiercely loyal to their ruler.[38] Also there was a body of watchmen (*vigiles*), 3500 strong, who served as an imperial fire brigade and as a kind of night police for prevention of petty crimes.[39] For more serious police work and for major crowd control there were the Urban Cohorts, 3000 strong, under a Prefect of the City. The commanders of these special forces were appointed by the Emperor and served at his pleasure.[40]

The Empire itself nearly defied description. Teeming with some fifty million souls of as many races and creeds as there are around the Mediterranean today, it was a hodgepodge of culture, climate and geography. North Africa was fertile in the Roman period, producing grain, fruits and vegetables in great abundance.[41] Egypt was naturally a special case, fed as it was by the Nile, snaking through the land with its life-giving water and fecund alluvial deposits. People of all sorts – Greeks, native Egyptians and Jews – lived in Alexandria, a city bursting with doctrinal and ethnic passions. Egypt was rich and became a major source of grain for Roman bread. The two legions stationed there, mainly to keep the population docile rather than to defend the frontiers, were a small price to pay for the bounty of the Nile.[42]

The eastern Mediterranean was more of a problem. Necessary strategically for defence against the Parthians, it was also economically and culturally a productive region, particularly Syria (including ancient Phoenicia).[43] But Palestine was often a source of trouble; the Jews living there were the most rebellious of Rome's subjects anywhere in the Empire. From Augustus to Caligula Roman emperors tried to dominate the region with a combination of force and diplomacy, using when possible the Jewish house of Herod the Great as an intermediary between Rome and the Jews.[44] Always, to the east, the Arsacid kings of Parthia kept a watchful eye on Rome's frail eastern frontier, and the heirs to Babylonian, Assyrian and Persian greatness in Mesopotamia sometimes harassed Rome's legions with their vaunted mounted archers.

Asia Minor, roughly modern Turkey, was a peculiar mixture of nearly barbarous robber-tribesmen and hillpeople in the mountainous central sections (especially in Galatia and in the high country of Cilicia, a district sometimes known as Isauria). On the other hand, the province of Asia in the western sector of Asia Minor was one of the jewels of the Roman Empire, rich, highly civilized, culturally productive. Generally the entire coastal strip, from Tarsus in the south-east all the way round to the north, bordering on the Black Sea, was productive and peaceful.[45]

BRITAIN

LOWER GERMANY

●Cologne

Elbe

BELGICA

LUGDUNENSIS

Rhine

UPPER
GERMANY   RAETIA   NORICUM

●Lyon   PANNONIA

AQUITANIA

NARBONENSIS   *Po*   DALMATIA

ALPS

TARRACONENSIS

LUSITANIA   CORSICA   ●Rome

BAETICA   ●Naples

SARDINIA   EP

TINGITANA   CAESARIENSIS   SICILY

M A U R E T A N I A   Carthage●

AFRICA

22

THE ROMAN EMPIRE UNDER CALIGULA

Extent of Empire

Provincial Boundary

—N—

Danube

ESIA

THRACE

EDONIA

ASIA

Ephesus

Athens

HAEA

CRETE

PONTUS
AND BITHYNIA

GALATIA

CAPPADOCIA

COMMAGENE

LYCIA

CILICIA

Antioch

Euphrates

Tigris

ARMENIA

Artaxata

P A R T H I A

Seleucia

CYPRUS

SYRIA

JUDAEA

Jerusalem

Alexandria

ARABIA

CYRENE

EGYPT

Nile

In the Early Roman Empire Greece and Macedonia had fallen from their former, high status in the world, but Greece especially retained some of the prestige attached to its earlier cultural attainments. Athens was a premier university city, a showcase of culture and learning.[46] To the north, under Augustus, Roman legions had pushed all the way to the Danube, where, along the banks of that great river, the province of Moesia (later Upper and Lower Moesia) was organized. Since the legions were normally stationed there along the frontier, Macedonia and Greece had to endure no overt military garrison. Legions on the upper Danube, mainly in Pannonia, also contributed to the military security of the area.[47]

In the West Gaul and Spain were major centres of Roman might and wealth.[48] Under Augustus Spain was finally pacified, although Roman legions continued to be stationed there throughout our period. Southern Spain (Baetica) was prosperous and civilized, producing in the age of Augustus and his heirs the great family of the Senecas, one of whom, Lucius Annaeus Seneca, emerged as one of Rome's greatest intellectual and literary figures after Cicero. The relationship between Caligula and Seneca was a tortured one,[49] but, for a time in the days of Nero, Seneca gained more political influence than anyone else in the Roman Empire. Still, the Senecas are simply representative of Spain's rise in the Roman world. Its mineral and agricultural wealth, as well as its flourishing southern cities, gave it a prominence in the Mediterranean it would not regain until the Age of Exploration in the New World.

The provinces of Gaul were the showpiece of Roman rule in the West. Conquered relatively late in Roman history in a famous campaign by Julius Caesar, Gaul was rapidly Romanized. Nature had bequeathed to the Gauls a marvellously effective network of navigable rivers, as well as a generally productive land. In the age before railways and other modern means of transportation, movement over water was cheap and effective; the great rivers of Gaul were an important asset.[50] Roman administrative organization served as a catalyst to expansive growth and development of the regional economy.

Across the Channel lay Britain. Caesar had been there twice during the Gallic War (in 55 and 54 BC) but was not able to make the far northern island a permanent Roman territory, despite his claim to have put it under tribute. The Emperors Augustus and Tiberius made no effort to extend Rome's frontier into the dripping mist of that wild Celtic land, but Romans had been captivated by the romantic nature of the great Caesar's daring. The poet Horace and others looked forward to the ultimate conquest of the island. It became something of an imperial dream, and, as we have seen, Caligula toyed with the idea, though it was his successor Claudius who actually achieved Britain's incorporation into the Empire.[51]

This brief survey of the Roman Empire should be enough, I hope, to give some sense of the vast extent of Roman power, of the variety and vitality of that tremendous Empire, put together by the crafty hands of those two sage and responsible administrators, Augustus and Tiberius. Soon we must consider the dramatic situation in which a young man of twenty-four, with the instincts but not the training for imperial rule, found himself, in uncontested possession of all that power. It would not be long before he told the two consuls, reclining next to him at a banquet, 'You know, don't you, that with one nod from me I could have your throats cut right now?'[52] It was true, of course, but an emperor with somewhat more sagacity would never have mentioned it.

The Julio-Claudian Dynasty

Republican Rome was as much an aristocracy as it was a republic, and it had produced many great and famous families: the Scipios, Fabians, Claudians, Cornelians, and Valerians, to name but a few. The emperorship was created when one of those families, the Julian, gained complete control of the government, ultimately in collusion through intermarriage with another, the Claudian. The Julio-Claudian dynasty is as fascinating as any in history, and the popular appeal of Augustus, Tiberius, Caligula, Claudius and Nero can compete even with the Tudor line and Henry VIII's wives.[53]

Caligula was the first Roman emperor who had large proportions of both Julian and Claudian blood in his veins. He was also the first Roman emperor who was born a prince, from birth a member of the ruling dynasty.[54] Augustus' birth was actually relatively obscure. Not until his adoption by the will of Julius Caesar did he achieve major recognition. Tiberius (Tiberius Claudius Nero) was born a Claudian, and it was not until his adoption by Augustus in AD 4, when Tiberius was forty-five years old, that he became definitively and irrevocably the heir to imperial power. On the other hand, when Caligula was born in AD 12, his father Germanicus was already the adopted son of Tiberius and heir-designate to the throne. From birth Caligula was truly a prince, though he had elder brothers who might stand in his path to the emperorship.[55]

Although the Julio-Claudian line is a famous one, and its individual members are historically significant, the family was very large, and the reader might understandably be confused by all the names. Since Caligula played such an important role in the history of the family, however, since he owed his initial prominence and even his claim to the throne to his place in it, rather than to talent and achievement, and since other members of the family were to be key actors during the course of his reign, we must examine briefly its colourful figures.

Julius Caesar was the founder of the dynasty, though it was his grandnephew, Gaius Octavius (63 BC – AD 14), who later became known as Octavian and then as Augustus, who is usually regarded as Rome's first emperor.[56] Caesar's greatness had burst explosively upon the Roman world, and it is perhaps accordant with the tumultuous nature of his dictatorship that the regime ended, as it began, in a grave crisis, a stunning assassination that left Caesar's contemporaries staggering in disbelief and unprepared for a future that did not include the triumphant hero. After the Ides of March, 44 BC, Mark Antony, one of the conqueror's closest associates, tried manfully to fill the void,[57] but Caesar's will had created a new power-broker in the eighteen-year-old Gaius Octavius, Caesar's obscure grandnephew, who was named primary heir and adopted son by the Dictator. Adoption by will was not an uncommon Roman practice.

The young Octavius took his adoptive father's name and was known to his contemporaries as Caesar, but modern historians usually call him Octavian from his new full name, Gaius Julius Caesar Octavianus. In the period from 43 to 30 BC the so-called Second Triumvirate ruled Rome, a committee consisting of Antony, Octavian and Lepidus, the weakest of the three, who fell out of the competition for power in 36 BC. Octavian, in control of Rome's western provinces and of Italy, manoeuvred Antony and the flamboyant general's lover and political associate, Cleopatra, into the war that ended with the Battle of Actium (31 BC) and the suicides of the couple in Egypt the following year.[58] Octavian became sole ruler of the Roman Empire, and a few years later, in 27 BC, after he had reorganized the government, he was given the name Augustus, meaning 'revered' or 'holy', in recognition of his services to the state.

As the first emperor of Rome Augustus developed a dynastic policy. He was anxious to see power pass peacefully from his own hands to an heir from his family in order to avoid the chaos of civil war on his death and to stabilize power during his lifetime. There was, however, one serious complication: the new Emperor had no son. By an earlier marriage to a disconsolate, moralistic woman named Scribonia Augustus had a daughter, Julia (39 BC – AD 14), who figured prominently in his dynastic schemes, although as a woman patriarchal Romans would not have considered her a possibility for the throne in her own right. Since 38 BC Augustus had been married to Livia (58 BC – AD 29), an intelligent, beautiful and strong-willed woman who survived well into her eighties.[59] By a previous marriage to a member of the Claudian family Livia had two sons, Tiberius (42 BC – AD 37) and Drusus (38–9 BC). This Drusus was the father of one emperor, Claudius, and the grandfather of another, Caligula, so his place in the Julio-Claudian line was eventually very prominent, although he fell from a horse and died before his descendants achieved their illustrious stature.[60] For a while, even though they were stepsons of the Emperor, Tiberius and Drusus were not considered likely candidates for the succession, since they had no Julian blood.

On the other hand Augustus had a sister, Octavia (?–11 BC). She had once been married, from 54 to 40 BC, to a Gaius Marcellus, a man who as consul in 50 BC had strongly opposed Julius Caesar, though Caesar later pardoned him. By this high-ranking senator Octavia bore a son, Marcus Marcellus, who as nephew of the Emperor with Julian blood in his veins (through his mother) became a popular young prince in Rome, a favourite of the people and of Augustus. Marcellus married the ruler's daughter, Julia, in 25 BC and seemed the most likely person to become Rome's next leader.[61] Actually, by a later marriage to Mark Antony, arranged at the time of an attempted reconciliation between him and Octavian, Octavia produced two children whose role in the Julio-Claudian family was ultimately more important: Antonia Major married L. Domitius Ahenobarbus, and they were the grandparents of the future Emperor Nero as well as of Messalina, wife of Claudius; Antonia Minor married Tiberius' brother Drusus, and they were the parents of Germanicus and Claudius and the grandparents of Caligula. Ironically then, through Octavia's marriage with Antony, there was as much of his blood in the Julio-Claudian line – more, actually – as there was of Augustus.[62]

Although the family tree is complicated with numerous branches, as any reader of Robert Graves knows, most of the characters are important in one way or another. Their interrelationships will compound and confuse the reign of Caligula. Another major figure, a maternal grandparent of Caligula, was the lifelong confidant and satellite of Augustus, the famous general and statesman, Marcus Agrippa.[63] Agrippa was a childhood friend of the Emperor and always at his side, a strongman whom Augustus trusted and relied upon. He was not of senatorial birth (a fact that later galled Caligula), so he lacked the social background one might expect in an imperial heir. And, since he was the same age as Augustus, he was not ideally suited to stand in the line of succession. Nevertheless, Agrippa was handsome, hale and hearty, while the frailness of Augustus' health added urgency to his dynastic schemes.

The unexpected, premature death of Marcellus in 23 BC put Agrippa in the spotlight. Augustus needed him more than ever, and in 21 the closeness of the relationship between the two political giants was cemented by the marriage of Agrippa to the Emperor's daughter, Julia. Their union was a productive one; they had five children, including Caligula's mother, Agrippina the Elder. The others were Gaius and Lucius, whom Augustus actually adopted as his own sons and who are, therefore, commonly known as Gaius and Lucius Caesar; another daughter, the ultimately infamous Julia the Younger; and a son born after Agrippa's death, hence called Agrippa Postumus.

The unexpected death of Agrippa in 12 BC subverted Augustus' dynastic policy. The Emperor had hoped that Agrippa would live long enough to see Gaius and Lucius safely onto the throne, but in fact both were still mere youths when the general died. In the meantime, new arrangements had to be made for the succession. Eventually Augustus selected his dour and aristocratic elder stepson, Tiberius, though there is at least some evidence that the two did not get along very well.[64] But Tiberius had already served with distinction in various capacities in the imperial government. He became increasingly talented as an administrator and general as the years went by. He was forced to divorce a woman he loved to marry Julia, widow of Marcellus and Agrippa. The marriage floundered within a year or so, and Julia went on to become involved in a tragic sex scandal (2 BC) that led to her banishment, divorce from Tiberius, and estrangement from her father, who actually added a codicil to his will, prohibiting her ashes from being placed in his mausoleum. Julia died in exile and disgrace in AD 14 – starved to death, some say, by her bitter former husband, the new Emperor, Tiberius.[65]

After the temporary falling out with Augustus, when Tiberius spent a few years in a retirement that turned into forced exile on the island of Rhodes (6 BC – AD 2), and after the premature deaths of Lucius (AD 2) and Gaius (AD 4), Livia effected a reconciliation between the Emperor and his stepson. In fact Augustus had little choice. Most of the adult male members of his family had died. Tiberius knew the Empire and could govern it. So, in a famous settlement in AD 4, after the death of Gaius Caesar,[66] Augustus adopted Tiberius as his son, and from that moment on to the day of the great Emperor's death in AD 14 there was no doubt that Tiberius would become the next ruler. Actually, by the time of the death and subsequent deification of Augustus, Tiberius was effectively Co-Emperor and was firmly in control of the government.[67]

But the settlement of AD 4 had various ramifications, and they were crucial to the career of the – as yet unborn – future emperor, Caligula. Augustus made two other dynastic and family arrangements in that epochal year. He also adopted his surviving grandson, Agrippa Postumus, who was sixteen years old at the time. However, Postumus was a wild and unruly youth, possibly insane, certainly temperamental, hot-tempered, and physically strong, which made his fits of temper frightening. The youth was in no way suitable for the throne, and Augustus made it clear that of the two adoptions of AD 4 that of Postumus was for family reasons whereas the adoption of Tiberius was 'for the sake of the state'.[68] In short, Postumus was not to be in the line of succession, and two years later he found himself in banishment for having threatened Livia. On the death of Augustus he was murdered in his prison – whether on the orders of Augustus, Livia or Tiberius is unknown.[69] Slightly earlier, in AD 9, the Younger Julia, Postumus' sister, daughter of the Elder Julia, was banished for sexual misconduct in the tradition of her mother.[70] In the last few years of the reign of Augustus, at the time when Caligula was born, his mother Agrippina was the only one of the surviving children of Marcus Agrippa and Julia to occupy a prominent place in Roman public life.

Agrippina was married to Germanicus, son of Tiberius' dead brother, Drusus, and of Drusus' wife, Antonia, who was herself the daughter of Mark Antony and Augustus' sister, Octavia. Caligula's parents, then, Germanicus and Agrippina, both had Julian blood in their veins, but even more important than that was the fact that in AD 4 Augustus had required Tiberius to adopt Germanicus although Tiberius had a son of his own. So Germanicus, by virtue of the adoption, stood next in the line of succession after Tiberius. In the years after AD 4 Germanicus became the most popular Roman hero of his day. The historian Tacitus was so impressed with him that he compared him with Alexander the Great.[71] When Caligula was born in AD 12, the infant was a true prince, son of a popular future emperor, or so it was believed, and on both mother and father's side the descendant of the proud dynasty created by Caesar and Augustus.

There was, however, from the outset a dark shadow hovering over the imperial family. The mother and sole surviving brother and sister of Caligula's mother, Agrippina, lived in banishment, suffering miserably at the hands of Augustus and Tiberius. Agrippina almost certainly sympathized with those forlorn members of her immediate family, and the young princess had immense influence over her husband, Germanicus. There was only one solution to this dynastic quagmire. As long as Augustus and Tiberius lived, there could be no hope for the exiled Julians, but if both should die, or more particularly if Tiberius should die, since Augustus had entered a decrepit senility anyway, Germanicus would ascend the throne.[72] Agrippina could then secure the recall of her mother, brother and sister. Of course Tiberius did not die, and Agrippina's brother was murdered, and her mother was either starved on Tiberius' orders or committed suicide, according to another account.[73] The Younger Julia eventually died (AD 28) on a prison island off the coast of Italy. Furthermore, as we shall see in the next chapter, Agrippina's own relationship with Tiberius, probably never very good, deteriorated drastically in the early part of his reign. She too ultimately starved to death, imprisoned on the island of Pandateria (AD 33).

One need not indulge in armchair psycho-history to wonder how these passionate dynastic tensions affected the young Caligula. On the one hand a child of destiny, on the other an important player in a dangerous game, the youthful prince was surrounded by victims as well as by beneficiaries of the new regime, both within his own family. How to show love to the objects of terror without bringing terrorism on oneself is a problem many have faced in the totalitarian regimes of the twentieth century. It was not unknown in the tyrannies of antiquity. Although Caligula's case was not unique, the forces swirling around him were extreme by any standard.

2. The Young Caligula

Caligula's earliest years, from infancy to age seven, were tumultuous and extraordinary. Assuming that the young prince was not born with genetic disorders that affected his mental equilibrium, he grew up from birth in an environment that shattered all sense of psychological security. As a two-year-old lad he was trapped in a rebellion of his father's legions along the Rhine and whisked about in panic and frenzy when no one knew how far things would get out of hand. A few years later when he was seven, his father, the great Germanicus, died 'under mysterious circumstances in Syria at the other end of the Roman Empire. Caligula was there. In those first, formative years of his life, he had travelled everywhere with his mother and father and had witnessed events that shook the Roman world. Small wonder then that they also shook him.

Even the peacetime experiences of those tender, early years would have been enough to affect the composure of a quite normal person. The great parades, the military guards, the thronging crowds of people who assembled wherever the popular Germanicus went, all the trappings of the new imperial dynasty created by the immortal Augustus, would have turned many young heads. Caligula was not in fact heir-designate, since he had two elder brothers, and perhaps Germanicus and Agrippina were less inclined to subject him to the rigorous discipline and training Augustus had imposed on Gaius and Lucius Caesar. If Caligula was actually 'spoiled' by his parents, and there is some evidence that he was, the combination of imperial grandeur and parental indulgence could have been devastating, to say nothing of the traumas of legionary rebellion and the death of Germanicus.

We know from a letter quoted in Suetonius' *Life of Augustus* that even the Emperor took an active interest in the baby prince. Writing in AD 14 to Caligula's mother, Augustus said:

Yesterday I made arrangements for Talarius and Asillius to bring your son Gaius to you on the eighteenth of May, if the gods will. I am also sending with him one of my slaves, a doctor who, as I have told Germanicus in a letter, need not be returned to me if he proves of use to you. Good-bye, my dear Agrippina! Keep well on the way back to your Germanicus.[74]

Germanicus had left for the Rhine by early AD 13, immediately after his consulship in 12.[75] Agrippina probably went with him, leaving Caligula behind to be cared for in the house of Augustus.[76] That means that the infant did not see his parents for about eighteen months, and it is possible that the psychological effects of early childhood separation stayed with him for the rest of his life.[77]

Nothing else is known about the infancy of Caligula until the famous events in the legionary camps along the Rhine in the last months of AD 14, after the death and deification of Augustus and the accession of Tiberius. Caligula had left Rome on 18 May, and the journey to the Rhine probably took about eighty days, a difficult trip for a two-year-old.[78] He must have arrived at about the moment of Augustus' death on 19 August, just in time to witness a frightening mutiny of the legions under his father's command. His reunion with his parents after an eighteen-month separation was a turbulent one.

Germanicus had been governor in Gaul for about a year, conducting the census and assessing taxes, when the four legions of Lower Germany rose up in a dangerous mutiny, hoping that the beginning of the new regime of Tiberius offered an occasion to secure some concessions.[79] Angry at what they considered to be unjust conditions of service, older soldiers wanted their discharge and pensions, while the younger ones demanded more pay and release from heavy work-details. All complained of the harsh discipline imposed by the centurions, and some of the hotheads turned mutiny into open treason by calling upon Germanicus to topple the new Emperor, Tiberius.[80] Their general, Aulus Caecina Severus, proved a feeble incompetent, and some centurions were lashed and beaten as a senseless fury took possession of the army.

Germanicus never wavered in his support of Tiberius. The heir-designate took an oath of loyalty, administered it to others around him and rushed to the legionary camps to suppress the revolt. In fact, despite Germanicus' loyalty, the relationship between the prince and Tiberius was probably strained. Their personalities were totally different. Germanicus was friendly, and he courted the favour of the people; Tiberius was grim and disdainful of his popular reputation. As one modern historian has said, 'It was simply a misfortune for Tiberius and for Rome that he and the successor chosen for him by Augustus were in temper utterly incompatible.'[81] Agrippina did not get along with Tiberius' mother, Livia, and there were other dynastic reasons why the legionaries might have believed that an appeal to Germanicus against Tiberius had some chance of success. But for whatever reason, Germanicus decided that his own time had not yet come, and he remained outwardly decisively loyal to his adoptive father.[82]

When Germanicus rushed to the scene of the crisis, the troops met him outside the camps. As he approached them, they seemed deferential, but as soon as he entered their ranks, they began to shout out their grievances. Some of the older soldiers reached for his hand, pretending to kiss it, but then jammed his fingers into their mouths to show that they had lost their teeth and deserved their discharges. As they broke ranks, Germanicus ordered them to reform, but they refused. An ugly situation was narrowly averted when the standard-bearers slowly began to come forward, and the troops fell in behind them. Then Germanicus gave a speech about the strength and stability of the Empire, but the army continued its grumbling. Soldiers pointed to their scars, inflicted by the severe system of military discipline, and complained about hard work, long hours and wretched pay. The old soldiers, especially, shouted out, 'Give us rest.'[83]

One of the main complaints of the troops was that they had not been paid the money Augustus had left them in his will. They asked Germanicus to pay it and again made clear their willingness to follow him to Rome and help him seize the throne. But the Prince shouted out that death was better than treason, drew his sword and threatened to commit suicide. Some of the men nearby made an effort to stop him, but others urged him on; one soldier even offered his own sword, saying that it was sharper.[84] To many this seemed outrageous, and the shock of it served to calm the mutineers somewhat, enabling Germanicus' friends to get him out of the way of immediate danger and back into his tent.

There was some concern that the rebellion might spread to the legions of Upper Germany, and also that the German barbarians on the other side of the Rhine might take advantage of the unrest to launch an invasion, particularly since Roman troops on the Danube were also mutinous.[85] In order to forestall any further deterioration of the situation, Germanicus decided to make a dramatic gesture. He forged a letter, pretending that it had been sent by the Emperor, and in it conceded discharges to everyone with more than twenty years' service. According to the letter, the legacies left by Augustus were to be doubled.[86] The suspicious rebels then demanded that these concessions be implemented immediately. Under these threatening circumstances Germanicus and his staff decided to use their personal travelling funds to pay the troops, and discharges were rapidly arranged until finally the men marched away under the commanders in a semblance of order. The historian Tacitus observed that it was 'a scandalous march – Eagle, standards, and the cash stolen from the commander, all were carried along together.'[87]

Germanicus' ruse did have a calming influence on the troops, and permitted him to move on to Upper Germany where the legions were restless but not yet mutinous. There he made the same concessions in discharges and money. This, combined with the quick execution of some troublemakers, quelled the attempt ·of some legionaries to start trouble and enabled Germanicus to return to the area around modern Cologne in Lower Germany, where two legions were chafing under the suspicion that the settlement reached with Germanicus might be nullified by a senatorial delegation that had recently arrived in the winter camp. It had been sent originally on the ceremonial mission of offering condolences to the general for the death of Augustus. The head of the delegation was an ex-consul, the aristocrat Lucius Munatius Plancus, who was considered a hard-nosed senator, opposed to negotiating with the legions. One night hostility and anger led to rioting, and Plancus narrowly escaped death at the hands of a military mob.

The next morning Germanicus addressed the troops and cowed the rioters. Plancus and other members of the delegation were escorted from the camp, and Germanicus was under some considerable pressure to send away his wife Agrippina and young son Caligula. Although Agrippina resisted leaving, she finally yielded to her husband's pleading and agreed to go with the boy. It was a sorry sight – the wife and son of an imperial prince threatened by the Empire's own soldiers. As Tacitus said, 'The scene suggested a captured city rather than a highly successful Caesar in his own camp.'[88] The women around Agrippina were frightened and crying; as they scurried about in a state of hysteria brought on by anxiety, some of the soldiers noticed the commotion and were overcome with shame at what they had done.

Germanicus took advantage of the agitation to excoriate the insurgents in the legions. While most of the troops urged him to allow his wife and son to remain with them and to save them from impending disgrace, he cried out that they should remove the criminals from their ranks. He agreed to let Caligula return to camp, but Agrippina was nearing the end of term in a pregnancy, and she had to leave.[89] Again Caligula was separated from his mother, and this time in frightening circumstances.

37

Immediately the troops set about to butcher the ringleaders of the mutiny, and in a glut of bloodshed the episode ended as quickly as it had begun. It is likely that Caligula witnessed some of the slaughter. Germanicus then moved against the other two legions of Lower Germany in their winter camp at Vetera, prepared to use force if necessary to quell the remaining mutineers. But before he arrived, the legionaries followed the example of their fellows at Cologne and killed the worst malcontents without even the semblance of a military trial.[90] There is no evidence that Caligula accompanied his father.

For a brief while, the mutiny on the Rhine had been exciting, and if it had spread to the legions of Upper Germany, there would have been eight rebellious legions altogether out of a total for the whole Empire of twenty-five. In fact three additional legions along the Danube in Pannonia had mutinied for higher pay and discharges, although not against the Emperor. Tiberius' son Drusus suppressed this rebellion somewhat more decisively than Germanicus had done on the Rhine and without making any concessions.[91] Still, there had been a momentary crisis of potentially great significance, and especially in the camp at Cologne, where the troops rioted, a very fleeting possibility of violence and bloodshed.

Here, far from Rome on the German frontier, the infant Caligula had played his first role in history. The child was only two years old when Augustus died and could not in later years have remembered the dramatic moment when he was whisked away from the rioting troops in his mother's arms. Actually he had already become popular with the legions and had received his nickname, 'Little Boots'. Since he was regarded as something of a mascot by the soldiers, they were sobered and ashamed when they saw him frightened and in flight, and it was that change in mood, as we have seen, that had given Germanicus the chance to end the mutiny. Caligula returned to his father's headquarters while Agrippina went on to Gaul. Although Caligula would not have remembered this event, the story of how the two-year-old boy turned around a military and political crisis of earth-shattering importance must have been a favourite one in his family, and indeed it became a part of the Roman historical tradition. The path to megalomania began early in his life.

It is quite likely that Caligula stayed on during the rest of Germanicus' command on the Rhine. We know that Agrippina did, and that she gave birth to two of Caligula's sisters, Agrippina the Younger and Drusilla, at Cologne, when she returned after the crisis.[92] Germanicus remained on the German frontier for two more years after the mutiny, and they were eventful years. The troops had clamoured to be led against the Germans, largely because they hoped to avoid any punishment for the mutiny by showing their loyalty to Rome in a war with the barbarians. It was by now the autumn of AD 14, but, despite the lateness of the season, Germanicus agreed to the campaign, probably because he saw it as an effective way to put an end to all rebellious sentiment in the army.[93]

After bridging the Rhine the heir-designate led a fairly substantial army of about 25,000 into hostile territory where he caught the Germans by surprise. As the Roman army approached the settlements of the Marsi, Germanicus divided it into four, and over a radius of fifty miles the Roman units swept through the countryside, killing men, women and children and devastating the area. This was all done in the name of revenge for the terrible disaster suffered by the Roman general Varus against the Germans in the Teutoburg Forest just a few years earlier in AD 9. At that time three legions had been ambushed and massacred, and Varus committed suicide.[94]

As Germanicus returned to the Rhine with his army after his successful foray, the Germans attempted to draw him into a trap and repeat their earlier victory against Varus. This time, however, Germanicus got word of their plans and marched with his legions in a defensive square. When the Germans attacked, they were driven back and wiped out, and the Roman army returned to camp on the safe side of the Rhine, bolstered by victory in their expeditionary mission. For the most part

Germanicus had handled the crisis of AD 14 reasonably well. He had at least escaped with his reputation more or less unscathed. Although the Emperor Tiberius probably resented the concessions the Prince had made, and rescinded some of them later, Germanicus' popularity with the people in Rome remained remarkable.[95]

In the next two summers, AD 15 and 16, Germanicus undertook one of the greatest campaigns in Roman history in the hope of achieving the conquest of all Germany up to the Elbe. The ultimate failure of this invasion meant that the Rhine would remain Rome's north-western frontier for centuries and that Germany would never be Romanized. Yet Germanicus' forays were popular with the people in Rome because they appeared to be successful. In the capital it was widely believed that Tiberius was jealous of his adopted son's victories and forced the dashing Prince to abandon the German war out of envy, at a time when he was on the verge of conquering Germany's boggy forests.[96]

Whatever the motives and the hidden agenda of the Emperor may have been, the campaign of AD 15 was extraordinary. Arminius, the famous chief of the Cherusci, and the man who had been the architect of the German victory over Varus in the Teutoburg Forest, had since fallen on hard times in the struggle to maintain his ascendancy over the various tribes, even his own. The chief had been outmanoeuvred politically by his father-in-law, a man named Segestes, who favoured cooperation with the Romans. Despite their family relationship, the two German leaders had never been friendly. Arminius had simply seized Thusnelda, Segestes' daughter, and carried her away, although she was already betrothed to someone else. Segestes hated Arminius and often passed information on to the Romans about his son-in-law's plans. In Tacitus' words, 'What are bonds of love between united hearts became with bitter foes incentives to fury.'[97] In any event, Germanicus decided to take advantage of this dissension among the German leaders.

The Prince's strategy was to divide the three main German tribes, the Cherusci, the Chatti, and the Bructeri, and to attack and defeat them one at a time. He turned first against the Chatti. Because the spring of AD 15 was unusually dry, and the rivers were not swollen with flood waters, the Romans marched much faster than usual towards their foe. Taken by surprise, the Chatti had no chance of resistance. Women, children and the feeble were killed or captured, while the able-bodied men attempted a brief struggle, only to be quickly overcome. Some of the German warriors surrendered to Germanicus, while others simply disappeared into the forest. The Prince burned the tribal capital, ravaged the countryside, and marched back to the Rhine.[98] Another detachment of Germanicus' army under the general Caecina had prevented the Cherusci from rendering aid to the Chatti. Caecina had incompetently lost control of his army during the mutiny, but he delivered good service under Germanicus' guidance. The strategy of 'divide and conquer' was working.

Unfortunately, however, the power struggle among the Cherusci took a dangerous turn, one that the Romans had not anticipated. Arminius managed to gain control over the tribe by preaching war, and Segestes was forced to flee to Germanicus, who gave the Cheruscan leader a home in Roman Gaul. But now the Cherusci were firmly under the influence of their warleader and hero, the man who had led them to victory over Roman legions in the past.

Arminius rallied the Cherusci behind him by insulting Germanicus, pointing out that the great Augustus and Tiberius had failed to take Germany and that the young prince surely did not have their ability. An army of mutineers, Arminius said, had no chance against German fighters. As a result of this campaign of propaganda, the barbarian leader gained widespread support, not only in his own tribe but throughout Germany. He succeeded in mobilizing a force of united tribes in the war against Rome, and Germanicus' situation, which had seemed so promising, now looked threatened.[99] The Roman commander took immediate steps to prevent the coalescing of the tribes by moving from opposite directions against the Bructeri. The attempt to trap this major German tribe in a pincer-movement depended upon a coordinated effort by three separate Roman armies, the sort of thing the Romans did very well indeed. Training and discipline made it possible for them to execute the complicated manoeuvres that gave them their strategic and tactical advantages over the Germans.[100]

The Bructeri occupied the land in Germany roughly between the Ems and the Lippe, directly across the Rhine. Caecina moved with four legions along the southern border of their territory to the Ems. Another commander led cavalry down from Frisian lands, and Germanicus boarded four legions onto ships and sailed through what was later the Zuyder Zee to the mouth of the Ems river. As the invading Roman forces united, the Bructeri responded by burning their own land, but the strategy did not stay the advance of Germanicus' army. Indeed, a Roman cavalry commander actually found one of the three legionary standards lost with Varus' army.[101]

Germanicus then decided to find the site of the earlier Roman defeat and to give the remains of Varus and his men a decent burial. Eventually Varus' camp was discovered, six years after the battle, along with bones and broken weapons. Germanicus laid the first sod on the funeral mound. The remnants of the three lost legions were all treated with respect, and the Roman troops, far from losing heart in this highly emotional and poignant situation, renewed their wrath against the Germans. In the end, however, the Bructeri escaped by abandoning their territory and moving further east. The Emperor Tiberius was not happy to hear the news of the discovery of the Varian disaster, partly because he resented everything Germanicus did, partly because he feared it might demoralize the army, and partly because he considered any tampering with the former battlefield sacrilegious. The act must have captured the Roman imagination, however, and added to the considerable fame the Prince already had.[102]

In any event, Germanicus then turned against Arminius, who retreated to draw the Romans deep into the forest. There the

42

Germans attempted an ambush, but the army escaped after a close call. Germanicus divided it into three parts again to return to the Rhine now that the summer campaigning season was over, but the force under Caecina was attacked and nearly destroyed. Caecina even had a nightmare in which the ghost of Varus lured him into a massacre. Arminius tried to repeat his earlier victory, and thought he had a chance when the Romans panicked, but the Germans were so anxious for booty that they let the Romans get away.[103]

Because of a quarrel among German leaders, some of whom wanted to storm the Roman camp directly and take everything, rather than wait to attack the Romans from hiding places along their route of retreat, as Arminius had urged, Caecina beat off the German assault. He then led his army back to the Rhine where Agrippina had kept the bridge open, despite rumours of a German advance. We are told that she even stood at the end of the bridge praising the troops as they marched by. Tiberius considered this quite unwomanly behaviour and was suspicious of her ambition: 'Generals had nothing left them,' he thought, according to Tacitus, 'when a woman went among the companies, attended the standards, ventured on bribery, as though it showed but slight ambition to parade her son in a common soldier's uniform, and wish him to be called Caesar Caligula.'[104]

That part of the army under Germanicus eventually made it back to the Rhine, though it suffered quite heavy losses from storms and floods on the way. The campaign was treated as a great success. The Senate in Rome voted Germanicus a triumph and other honours, and it is likely that Tiberius hoped to put an end to any further campaigning across the Rhine by treating the recapture of the lost standard of the army of Varus as the goal.[105] If that was the Emperor's intention, Germanicus did not get the message, or, perhaps, he simply chose to ignore it. Instead, he planned another thrust into Germany for AD 16 and did not return to Rome to enjoy his recognition.

For this last great effort Germanicus hoped to eliminate some of the weaknesses of the Roman army on campaign in Germany. Compared with the primitive, non-existent logistical system of the enemy, the Roman supply train was magnificent, but it also slowed the army down, and in the often muddy, forested terrain of Germany, with heavy rains and short summers, the Roman convoy could be easily attacked. Germanicus decided to use naval power to overcome this disadvantage. In 15 he had not deployed enough ships, and some of his army was required to move overland. Transport vessels rather than warships were his greatest need, and the Prince used the winter to build the kind of fleet he would require in the waters off the German coast between the mouths of the Rhine and the Elbe.[106]

At this time Germany was in a state of turmoil. Rome had attempted to work her will in the country without actually occupying it, and the 'search and destroy' strategy used against the tribes had not been particularly effective. Over the winter Germans had moved back onto the Varian battlefield and destroyed the Roman monument there. More importantly, they had captured a number of Roman defence works on the German side of the Rhine. Despite the massacre of the Chatti just a year earlier, Germanicus had to send troops against them again in 16 before he could embark with the fleet for the mouth of the Ems. Finally, he was able to disembark, but inexplicably he landed on one side of the river and then bridged it to march for the Weser. Why he did not land his troops on the other bank is a mystery.[107]

When the Romans reached the Weser, they found the Cherusci under Arminius lined up for battle on the opposite bank. Germanicus did not want to fight before building bridges. One of the Roman advantages over the Germans, recognized since the days of Caesar, was military engineering, and it would have been foolish of Germanicus to have thrown that away. By the time the Romans crossed the river, Arminius had withdrawn to find a more suitable battlefield, and Germanicus learned from deserters that he planned a night attack on the Roman camp. Since Germanicus wanted to know the state of morale in his army, he put on a disguise and mixed with his men. He learned that they were confident in him and of their chance for victory. When the German attack came, it failed miserably. Realizing that the Romans were awake and on guard, the Germans simply retreated.[108]

The Roman army was deep in the heart of Germany, far from the safety of the camps along the Rhine. The next morning, to bolster spirits, Germanicus spoke to his men, telling them that they could use the forests and swamps against the Germans, that the Romans were better armed and better trained, and that the barbarians yielded quickly and easily to panic. Reminding his troops that the Elbe was now nearer than the Rhine and that they were not going beyond the Elbe, the Roman commander urged his men to get the job done. Arminius, for his part, also tried to inspire his men. He told them that the Roman troops were simply the cowards left over from Varus' army, that they had more wounds on their backs than anywhere else, and that they had invaded Germany by fleet because they were afraid to fight on land. The actual battle, on the plain of Idisavisto, probably somewhere east of Minden on the Weser, was easily won by the Romans, as almost all conventional battles with barbarians were, although it lasted all day, from nine in the morning to nightfall, because it took many hours to slaughter countless foe. Roman losses were insignificant.[109]

The Germans who survived, including Arminius, first considered a general withdrawal to the Elbe, but in their fury against Rome they decided to regroup and fight again. They tried to lay another ambush, but Germanicus' intelligence network discovered the scheme, and he moved quickly against them. They had boxed themselves in with a swamp in their rear and could not retreat. Again forced to fight a conventional battle, the Germans were at a disadvantage, and this time Germanicus urged his men on to kill everyone in sight, telling them that he wanted no captives, and that it was necessary to wipe out the Germans to end the war. After the battle Germanicus erected a monument with an inscription proclaiming that the army of the Emperor Tiberius had conquered Germany from the Rhine to the Elbe.[110]

It was tactful of him to mention Tiberius and to omit any reference to his own name, but it did not placate Tiberius, who was increasingly anxious for his heir-designate's return from Germany and an end to adventurism beyond the Rhine.

The return of the victorious Roman army to the camps on the Rhine proved a calamity. Part of the army returned overland, but by far the greater part was placed on the newly constructed transport fleet and moved down the Ems to the sea. According to Tacitus, 'At first the calm waters merely sounded with the oars of a thousand vessels or were ruffled by the sailing ships',[111] but soon a great storm with thunderous hail and mighty gales dispersed the fleet: 'Horses, beasts of burden, baggage, were thrown overboard, in order to lighten the hulls which leaked copiously through their sides, while the waves too dashed over them.'[112] Some ships sank, and Germanicus' command ship was driven by the storm into the territory of the Chatti, where he was at first convinced that everything had been lost. But then ships began to come in, a few at a time, and troops were picked up along the coast. Some of the barbarians tried to win Roman favour or at least get ransom money for the return of soldiers, some from as far away as Britain.

To make sure that the Germans would not be inspired to take advantage of this misfortune by renewing the war, Germanicus sent a force against the Chatti and he led one himself against the Marsi. He had learned that the Marsi had one of the standards taken from Varus' army. Both these expeditions were successful, and Germanicus returned to the winter camp with the recaptured standard.[113] The Germans had been crushed and demoralized by this show of strength, but Germany had not been conquered. Without actual occupation of the land by Rome, the tribes would not yield to Roman domination. Whether Romans had the manpower at this time to attempt the occupation of Germany is debatable, and therefore the strategy of Germanicus has been questioned by modern scholars. Germanicus may have been wrong, but his forays had increased his popularity back in Rome with everyone except the Emperor.[114]

Although Germanicus acutely wanted to stay for another year to complete his efforts across the Rhine, Tiberius used every argument and blandishment to persuade him to come back to Rome. He said that losses had already been heavy, through no fault of the commander, that under Augustus more had been accomplished by policy than by arms, and that Arminius would hang himself if given enough rope. Besides, the Emperor offered Germanicus a second consulship but indicated that the Prince needed to come to Rome to serve in person. Finally he appealed to the strong friendship that existed between Germanicus and Tiberius' own son Drusus, Germanicus' brother by adoption. The Emperor said that Germanicus had already attained sufficient glory; any more should be left to his brother, Drusus. Under this relentless pressure from Rome Germanicus had little choice, and he reluctantly agreed to return to the capital where he would finally celebrate his triumph.[115]

What had happened to Caligula during these dangerous two years on the Rhine? We know very little. The only reference in ancient literature to this phase of his life is the one quoted above from Tacitus about Agrippina standing at the bridge greeting the troops on their return from the campaign of 15. The fact that Tiberius resented the way Agrippina paraded Caligula about in a soldier's uniform, encouraging the troops to call him Caesar Caligula, is significant. Already the animosity that later inflamed relations between Agrippina and the Emperor had begun, and it focused on her ambition for her husband and her sons, including Caligula, the youngest of the three boys. Probably, since the other two were almost certainly in Rome, her treatment of Caligula was a special concern of the Emperor.

Although Caligula was only four years old when Germanicus and Agrippina left the Rhine, he had witnessed some great events and was learning of his own and his family's importance. We can only speculate as to what impression that left on him, but almost at the age of five, beginning to experience things he would remember for the rest of his life, the remarkable events surrounding his father must have had a strong influence on him.

47

On 26 May AD 17 Germanicus Caesar celebrated his triumph over the Germans.[116] Caligula rode with his brothers and sisters in the great commander's chariot. An enormous crowd gathered for the occasion, and the enthusiasm of the Roman people for their heroic prince and his family was nearly boundless. Tiberius gave every member of the city *plebs* three hundred sesterces in Germanicus' name, an enormous figure, since an annual subsistence salary for a family of four was something in the neighbourhood of one thousand sesterces. Possibly the famous Grand Cameo of Paris – today in the Bibliothèque Nationale – represents Tiberius' reception of Germanicus on his return from the Rhine.[117] If so, the figures behind Germanicus are Agrippina and the young Caligula.

It does not take much imagination to see that a five-year-old, on whom was lavished the unrestrained attention of the multitude, might see his own place in the world as somewhat greater than that of the common man. Although there is very little evidence, what does exist indicates that his mother Agrippina enjoyed and encouraged the attention the boy received and it is not unreasonable to assume, from what we know about her, that she also encouraged him to entertain grandiose thoughts of his own importance. It is a significant part of the tradition about Caligula that he was adored by those around him from infancy.

An entirely new phase of his early childhood began when his father was sent by the Emperor to the East to deal with an urgent crisis that involved the Parthians and Armenia and threatened the eastern frontier of the Roman Empire.[118] In AD 15 the Parthians had expelled their king, Vonones, who had been placed on the throne by the Emperor Augustus. Since Vonones had been friendly with Rome, and his successor, Artabanus III, had been selected by men who hated the pro-Roman policy, the situation was critical. Furthermore, Vonones had fled to Armenia at a time in AD 16 when the Armenian throne was vacant. The exiled Parthian king simply took over Armenia, but the Emperor Tiberius did not officially recognize him as the new king. Naturally, the Parthians were also concerned about the situation. The Governor of Syria, Creticus Silanus, saw the possibility of a dangerous war with Parthia and invited Vonones to Syria where he was detained under house arrest although he was treated with honour. The solution to this diplomatic entanglement was not entirely obvious.[119]

In the meantime, the eastern frontier was threatened by other problems. Cappadocia, in modern Turkey, had been a client kingdom, or allied satellite state, of the Roman Empire for about fifty years, under its king, Archelaus, who had recently died under suspicious circumstances during a trip to Rome. Tiberius then annexed the area and made Cappadocia a Roman province.[120] There were also problems in the neighbouring territories of Commagene and Cilicia where the client kings had recently died. Tiberius decided to send Germanicus; the Emperor himself was too old, and the issues were important enough to require the personal attention of the heir-designate. Besides, the crisis served as a wonderful pretext to bring Germanicus back from Germany by apparently promoting him to an even greater command.[121]

In fact Germanicus was voted an extraordinary position. He was given authority – greater than that of the provincial governors – over all the provinces of the eastern Mediterranean, although this command did not include Egypt. Yet Tiberius, as we know, did not really trust Germanicus, so he replaced the Syrian governor Creticus Silanus, a friend of Germanicus, with a stubborn, old senatorial aristocrat, Gnaeus Calpurnius Piso, known for his sharp tongue and his arrogance, and supported in all his idiosyncrasies by his equally aristocratic wife, Plancina, a close friend of Tiberius' mother, Livia.[122] Clearly Tiberius hoped that Piso would keep an eye on Germanicus, and it is likely, as Tacitus claims, that the Emperor even gave secret instructions to Piso to do just that. If so, he placed Piso and Germanicus in a hopeless situation.

By the beginning of the year 18, the year Germanicus and Tiberius served as consuls, Germanicus had started his trip to the

East. Again Agrippina and Caligula went with him, as they had in Gaul, and it was at the site of Augustus' great victory over Antony and Cleopatra at Actium that Germanicus assumed his consulship.[123] Indeed, the entire journey to the East took on the overtones of a triumphal procession. Germanicus was clearly revered by the population of the Roman Empire, and he was greeted by admiring crowds wherever he went. When he entered Athens, he flattered the Greeks, much to their delight. His tour through the Aegean included a stopover at Troy, where Romans believed that their own history began with the flight of Aeneas. In Lesbos Agrippina gave birth to Julia Livilla, the last of Germanicus' six children, and the residents of the island proceeded immediately to deify the Prince's consort for favouring them with the birth of her child.[124] Such extravagant shows of affection must have had some influence on the young Caligula. Augustus, at the age of five, had not been subjected to this kind of massaging of his ego. In the case of Caligula it had started almost from birth.

On the other hand, Piso had made a terrible impression as he travelled to his province of Syria. In Athens he abused the Greeks by pointing out their failures and reminding them of the times when they had supported Rome's enemies. He even implied that Germanicus had detracted from Roman honour by treating the Athenians with more courtesy than they deserved. Then he dashed across the Aegean to beat Germanicus to Syria and the eastern frontier. In his province he tried to gain the favour of the troops by relaxing discipline and removing the strictest of the officers and centurions. Plancina too courted the troops and was more outspoken than her husband in criticizing Germanicus and Agrippina. It was not long before the rumour began to spread through the army that Tiberius had given his blessing to the mistreatment of the Prince and his family.[125]

Germanicus decided to ignore Piso's insults, at least for a while, and to hasten on to Armenia where he crowned a popular candidate for the throne, Zeno. It proved a happy choice – Zeno ruled for a decade and a half. Then, after leaving the Armenian capital of Artaxata Germanicus dealt with Cappadocia and Commagene.[126] In fact, whatever one may say of Germanicus' command along the Rhine, and it has been condemned by many modern historians, the Prince did well in the East, dealing with problems that might have been difficult indeed. Unfortunately relations with Piso quickly went from bad to worse. The Governor of Syria had been ordered to send a body of troops to Armenia, and he had not done so. It was outright insubordination, and Germanicus could not ignore it. When the Prince finally met the Governor in Syria, north-east of Antioch, there were harsh words, and the two potentates parted in anger. Afterwards Piso openly ignored Germanicus and attended to his superior only perfunctorily.[127]

When the King of Parthia asked for a personal meeting with Germanicus, the Prince declined, presumably so as not to offend or provoke Tiberius, but the Roman did accede to another request from the Parthian, and he sent the former king, Vonones, who had been under arrest in Syria, to the province of Cilicia so he would not be near the Parthian frontier. This also offended Piso because Vonones had become a good friend of the Governor's wife, Plancina.[128]

Although this rather tricky matter of protocol had been handled well by Germanicus, he made a serious mistake in 19 when he decided to visit Egypt.[129] The Prince may have intended the tour simply as recreation, as Tacitus implies, but it was also clearly an official visit. Great crowds greeted him in Alexandria, where his grandfather, Mark Antony, was still popular, and the reception got so out of hand that Germanicus had to admonish the Alexandrians not to treat him and Agrippina with honours that would have been appropriate only for Tiberius and his mother, Livia.[130] It is possible that Germanicus was deified by the Egyptians, and he may have been proclaimed Augustus. While in Egypt, but not before he had taken a trip up the Nile to visit Egyptian antiquities, he received a letter from the Emperor, rebuking him for wearing Greek dress and criticizing him severely for entering Egypt without permission. Augustus had declared Egypt off limits for all senators and equestrians, but Germanicus had assumed that the restriction did not apply to him. Tiberius made it clear that it did. It is possible, although Tacitus does not say so specifically, that Agrippina and Caligula accompanied Germanicus.[131]

When the Prince returned to Syria, he found that Piso had overturned many of his orders, particularly ones designed to restore discipline to the army. The two powerful Romans quarrelled, but then Germanicus fell mysteriously ill. The Prince became convinced that he had been poisoned by Piso, and in the walls and floors of the house where he was living were found human remains, lead tablets with Germanicus' name on them, and incantations and spells, all part of curses designed to consign Germanicus' soul to the underworld.[132] He sent a letter to Piso, formally renouncing friendship, and ordering the Governor to leave the province. As the Prince's condition worsened, and death appeared inevitable, he asked his friends to seek vengeance against Piso and Plancina. He admonished them, 'Show the people of Rome her who is the granddaughter of Augustus, as well as my consort; set before them my six children.'[133] They swore they would avenge him, and he died on 10 October AD 19, after a whispered conference with Agrippina. He was thirty-three years old, and the ancient sources agree that he was handsome, kind, considerate and even-tempered. In the words of Tacitus, 'He inspired reverence alike by look and voice, and, while he maintained the greatness and dignity of the highest rank, he had escaped the hatred that waits on arrogance.'[134]

Thus died one of the most famous Romans of the imperial age. His nobility of character had made him popular, but modern historians have been largely critical of him, mainly on grounds of policy and strategy.[135] His campaigns in Germany may have been misdirected, yet they had ample precedents in the Augustan period, and he had been appointed to his command by the ageing Emperor before his death. Germanicus' loyalty to Tiberius remained firm throughout, even to the time of his death. His diplomatic mission in the East had been handled with skill, and on balance Germanicus has not been treated fairly by his modern critics. Tacitus was a passionate historian, but that does not mean that his praise for Germanicus was wrong, and it is not necessary to condemn the Prince in order to extol the Emperor. Their relationship was an impossible one, forced on them by Augustus when he adopted Tiberius in AD 4 and required Tiberius to adopt Germanicus, even though Tiberius had a son of his own.

The funeral took place in Antioch amid comparisons of the dead hero with Alexander the Great. There were conflicting accounts in antiquity about whether his body showed the signs of poisoning.[136] Agrippina embarked with Germanicus' ashes shortly after the funeral, accompanied by her children, including the seven-year-old Caligula. He was now without question old enough to have remembered later the details of the sorrowful journey to Rome with his grieving mother and the ashes of his father. Many honours were voted to the memory of his dead father, and Caligula must have witnessed many solemn ceremonies in celebration of his father's greatness. But there was anger as well as sadness in the entourage of Agrippina and in the populace at Rome where rumours of the complicity of Piso and Plancina, Tiberius and Livia, spread fast.

The story of the Prince's death had reached Rome gradually; it was a long way from Syria, and news came in over time, first that Germanicus was gravely ill, then that he seemed to be recovering, and finally that he was dead.[137] The emotions of the crowd swayed back and forth from sadness to elation and grief, always mixed with anger because of the stories about Tiberius and Livia. In situations such as this, rumours abound, and there was one that Germanicus would have restored the republic, had he lived. When Agrippina landed in southern Italy, at Brundisium, only a small escort was sent there to meet her by Tiberius; but Drusus, Tiberius' son, and Claudius, Germanicus' brother and the future Emperor, went down to join the funeral cortège.[138]

Eventually Tiberius actually issued a decree ordering the

people to be restrained in their grief.[139] He had been especially troubled by the excessive adoration shown Agrippina. The mob was still worked up to a frenzy because Piso had not returned to satisfy justice. As soon as he did arrive in the city, charges were brought against him, and the trial brought on a resurgence of public fury and excitement. A crowd gathered outside the Senate, and the possibility of a lynching was in the air.[140] The death of Germanicus unleashed violent forces in Roman dynastic politics. Caligula had witnessed the tragedy and the sorrow of his family, although in later years he benefited greatly from the legend that grew up around his father. Little could he have known, at the time, how dangerous his family's condition was, now that the Prince was dead. The misfortunes that soon befell his mother and elder brothers would leave a permanent scar on the young boy.

3. Agrippina and Sejanus

After the death of Germanicus, Agrippina was so bitter and angry that she could not conceal her emotions from Tiberius and his mother, Livia. Unfortunately her animosity came at a particularly impolitic time. Tiberius was greatly embarrassed by the scandal surrounding Germanicus' death. The Prince's friends brought charges against Piso, and eventually the impetuous Proconsul was hauled before the Senate, accused of poisoning and treason.[141] Since Tiberius had commissioned the Governor to watch over Germanicus, Piso naturally expected the Emperor's protection against the accusations, and Plancina, Piso's wife, relied heavily on her friendship with Livia. Tiberius probably wanted to save Piso but understood that the political cost would be enormous. As a result, he backed away indecisively. Sometimes he helped his friend, sometimes he did not. Much like President Nixon in a later period, who eventually sacrificed his closest advisers, Ehrlichman and Haldeman, during the Watergate crisis, Tiberius offended everyone by failing to support his ally and by being unwilling to condemn him.

Agrippina wanted clear-cut revenge. Her arrogance was great and probably compounded by her belief that her eldest son, Nero, thirteen years old at the time of his father's death, would eventually become Emperor, even though such a belief was unrealistic as long as Tiberius' son Drusus lived. The Nero in question was not the later notorious Emperor; this one died prematurely after foul play. It is doubtful that Tiberius would have promoted the interests of anyone over those of his own son, and since there was no law of succession, it was never entirely clear who would become Rome's next ruler. Obviously it did not hurt any candidate's chances to be the choice of the current Emperor. Agrippina probably put considerable faith in the fact that her son had Julian blood in his veins; after all, his father had been marked out for the purple by the divine Augustus. Agrippina's pride in her family caused Tiberius to be especially distrustful of her.

Piso returned very slowly from Syria to Rome. He stopped in Illyricum to see Tiberius' son Drusus, while he sent his own son on to the capital to wait on Tiberius, who greeted the young man, Marcus, with courtesy but without warmth. Eventually Piso, who had not been treated as well by Drusus as he had hoped, entered Rome and was welcomed by a large household following, to the great distress of the mob, which had idolized Germanicus.[142] The consuls called upon Tiberius to take the case *in camera*, but the Emperor refused, causing considerable anxiety for Piso, and referred the matter back to the Senate without prejudice. The beleaguered senator found it difficult to find colleagues who were willing to serve as his advocates. Everyone waited to see how Tiberius would react under the circumstances, because his actions would shape the outcome of the trial, even though he had refused to accept it on his own responsibility.

The Emperor actually gave the first speech in the case. He observed that Piso had been his friend and that Augustus had trusted him. Furthermore, he reminded the Senate that Piso's appointment in Syria had been granted by that body. Two days were allotted for the prosecution and three for the defence, with an interval of six days. The prosecutors accused Piso of turning the legions against Germanicus, of hating the Prince, and of poisoning him. In the end the most serious charge was that Piso had taken up arms after Germanicus' death to reclaim Syria, a charge that was certainly true. On the charge of murder even Tacitus, who was highly partial to Germanicus, noted that the evidence was absurd.[143]

A mob gathered outside the Senate House ready to lynch Piso

should he be acquitted. Under the circumstances, Plancina abandoned her husband and, still hopeful that Livia would intervene to save her, she threw herself on the Augusta's mercy. The next day Piso cut his throat, leaving behind a message for Tiberius, asking him to spare his sons. The Emperor did that with probable comfort, but he was much distressed and chagrined when he had to intervene a few days later to save Plancina at his mother's request. As far as the people were concerned, Tiberius confirmed their suspicions that he and his mother had contrived Germanicus' death. Fear spread that Agrippina and her children might also be in danger.[144]

Many motions were offered in the Senate to condemn Piso's memory, but Tiberius rejected most of them. He protected Piso's sons, but he also rewarded those who had secured the conviction. Agrippina had been outspoken in her hatred of Piso and his wife. The fact that Tiberius had softened the treatment of Piso and asked for pardon for Plancina created hard feelings in the imperial family against the Emperor and his mother. How Antonia, Germanicus' mother, reacted, is not known with certainty, but she must have been restrained considering the high respect in which Tiberius later held her. Nor do we know for certain how Caligula felt about these events, but we do know from later acts that he was close to his mother, and it is reasonable to assume that he shared her strong feelings.

The early years of the reign of Tiberius were especially significant for the rise of his close adviser, the Praetorian Prefect, Sejanus.[145] Sejanus ultimately had a huge effect on the family of Caligula and on the future Emperor himself. The wily courtier used his position as commander of the newly created Praetorian Guard to win the trust of Tiberius. The new commander, who reported daily to the Emperor, had the largest armed force in the vicinity of the capital.[146] As Sejanus' influence grew, his daughter was betrothed to a son of the future Emperor Claudius. Unfortunately Claudius' son died prematurely when he threw a pear in the air and choked on it as it fell back into his mouth. It seems somehow an appropriately Roman way to die.[147]

Although Sejanus had unbridled ambition, and eventually plotted and murdered to secure the throne, in the period immediately after the death of Germanicus and the trial of Piso it was Tiberius' own son Drusus who seemed to be destined to rule Rome. Tiberius had almost certainly always favoured Drusus over Germanicus anyway, and after the death of the Prince, Tiberius arranged for Drusus to become consul in the year 21. Then, blaming ill health, the Emperor retired to the area around Naples to allow his son to stand centre stage in the political life of the capital. Drusus actually managed affairs rather well and was immensely popular. If the new Prince lived more ostentatiously than others and seemed to enjoy parties in the capital somewhat too much, that at least was preferable to the secluded, whimsical life-style of his father, the Emperor. Drusus was not the only Roman to like wine, the theatre and gladiatorial combat, nor was his tendency to violence necessarily un-Roman. The culmination of Drusus' prominence came in 22, before Tiberius returned to Rome, when the proud father asked the Senate to confer the Tribunician Power on his son. Not even Germanicus had shared that with the Emperor.[148]

As events transpired, the elevation of Drusus became an obstacle to the ambition of Sejanus. The Praetorian Prefect had continued to win Tiberius' confidence, and the Emperor referred to Sejanus as 'the partner in my toils'.[149] Furthermore, there was bad blood between the two rivals. In a fit of temper the impetuous Drusus had once hit the Prefect in the face. Seeking revenge, Sejanus seduced Drusus' beautiful wife Livia, a sister of Germanicus. Convinced, as Tacitus says, that a woman, 'having parted with her virtue will hesitate at nothing', Sejanus then persuaded his lover to join him in a conspiracy to kill Drusus by poison.[150]

Regardless of the tensions generated in the imperial dynasty by the hostility of Agrippina, Tiberius, consistent with the wishes of Augustus, continued to regard the two elder sons of Germanicus, Nero and Drusus, as eventual heirs to the throne. How he would have arranged such a succession, no one knows, but probably he intended to require his own son Drusus to adopt Caligula's brothers just as Tiberius had adopted Germanicus. Drusus seemed to like the young men and may have been responsible for their care.[151]

It was possibly because Drusus' wife, Livia, favoured her own two sons over those of Germanicus and Agrippina that she conspired with Sejanus. In any event, Nero, at the age of fourteen the eldest of the sons of Agrippina, assumed the toga of manhood in the year 20 and was betrothed to the daughter of Drusus and Livia, Julia Livilla. In 23 the young Drusus, Nero's brother, assumed the toga of manhood. Both princes were given special dispensations permitting them to hold public offices five years before the legal minimum age, a privilege that had earlier been granted by Augustus to Tiberius. So Caligula's family remained in the limelight, though Caligula himself was only eleven years old in 23, and no one apparently considered him a possible successor. All the attention had been focused on his two elder brothers who had been groomed for the purple.[152]

Later in the same year, Sejanus and Livia poisoned Drusus, although he appeared to die from natural causes. It was not until several years afterwards that the truth came out. Tiberius continued to go to the Senate House even in the interval between Drusus' death and the funeral in order to immerse his sadness in the affairs of state. Before the Senate he asked the consuls to bring in the young Nero and Drusus, and the Emperor commended them to the Senate's care, pointing out that they had lost their father and their uncle. The brothers of Caligula now emerged as the leading young men in the state after the Emperor himself, who was at this time nearly sixty-five years old.[153]

The house of Germanicus seemed destined to rule after all. Agrippina foolishly could not restrain herself, however, and her ambition and arrogance fuelled the envy of Sejanus, who now looked upon Augustus' granddaughter and her two elder sons as his chief impediment to sole power.[154] The influence of the crafty Prefect proved equal to the challenge, as he demonstrated over the next few years. He managed to persuade the two Livias, the

Emperor's mother and his own lover, Drusus' widow, to accuse Agrippina of seeking imperial power for herself. Tiberius was willing to believe almost anything about Agrippina, and some of her own friends were suborned by Sejanus to provoke her into reckless statements. Still, the young Nero made quite an impression late in the year 23 when he gave a public speech on behalf of the cities of Asia for permission to build a temple to Tiberius, Livia and the Senate. His oratory reminded the audience of his father Germanicus. Sejanus fumed with resentment.[155]

Then, on 3 January AD 24, the priests included Nero and Drusus in the public prayers they said for the safety of the Emperor. Although they probably thought Tiberius would be pleased, he reacted in fury, regarding it as insulting to be treated as equal to such youths. He suspected Agrippina had put the priests up to it and was mollified only after they assured him in private meeting that she had not. Sejanus decided to take advantage of this opportunity, however, and argued before the Emperor that Agrippina's faction was ripping the state in two, laying the foundation for civil war. He then turned against two of the leading senatorial supporters of Germanicus and destroyed their careers, causing one of them to commit suicide while the other went into exile.[156]

In 25 Sejanus took the unusual step of asking Tiberius for permission to marry Drusus' widow, Livia. The scheming minister argued that Livia needed protection for her children against the ambition of Agrippina. Tiberius offered a studied reply. Agrippina might become more hostile if the proposed marriage split the Julio-Claudian family clearly into two factions. Furthermore, as Tiberius indelicately pointed out, Sejanus was not of senatorial birth, whereas Livia had previously been married to Gaius Caesar, adopted son of Augustus, and to Drusus, also an heir-designate to the throne. Everyone would object to such a match, even if the Emperor agreed to it, and Agrippina's behaviour would worsen. Tiberius said that friendship obliged him to speak openly, but he added that he would not stand in the way of the two lovers if they were determined to push ahead, although he indicated that great rewards were in store for Sejanus in the future if the loyal servant continued steadfast in his devotion to the Emperor.

The letter was a monumental sham, a masterpiece of subterfuge. Tiberius said openly and quite properly that the decision was not up to him. The two lovers could make their own decision. But at the same time the Emperor also said 'no' and said it emphatically. This refusal to accede to Sejanus' wishes does not necessarily imply any lack of trust in the imperial agent. After all, Tiberius' objections to the marriage made good sense. It would have caused trouble (more trouble than the Emperor suspected), and the aristocracy would indeed have resented the dynastic elevation of the equestrian upstart.[157]

Sejanus simply gave up the idea. Possibly Livia had been the main instigator in the first place, but the Prefect chose not to lose or endanger his present position and influence by aspiring too high and too fast. Instead he pursued another objective, and tried to persuade the Emperor to abandon Rome altogether, emphasizing the ugliness of life in the capital and the quiet repose of other beautiful and charming sites in the Empire. Sejanus knew that his own power would grow if Tiberius retired from Rome, and the Emperor had often spent long periods away from the city and seemed to enjoy being absent from the crowds and dynastic tensions.

In the meantime, Agrippina suffered another heavy loss when her cousin, Claudia Pulchra, widow of the famous Varus who had lost the three legions in Germany, was accused of adultery and of attempting to poison the Emperor and to destroy him with sorcery. Agrippina was outraged by the accusations. Claudia Pulchra's son was engaged to Agrippina's daughter, and the Princess went directly to the Emperor to intervene. She found him in an act of piety, offering sacrifices to the divine Augustus. Overcome by fear and anger, she indignantly noted the irony of worshipping a man on the one hand and destroying his descendants on the other. This outburst did not please the

61

Emperor. He took Agrippina by the hand and said to her, 'Do you think life has been unfair to you, because you are not Empress of Rome?'[158] Tiberius allowed Claudia Pulchra to be convicted and praised her accuser.[159]

Agrippina lost heavily in this affair, and not much later, while she was still enraged by it, Tiberius visited her when she was ill, and she asked him to give her another husband. Since her sons were still the heirs-designate, such a marriage would have strong political undertones. For essentially the same reasons that he opposed the marriage of Livia with Sejanus, he was not going to suffer Agrippina to marry anyone. The two imperial widows would not be allowed to find champions for their sons, because the husbands of the princesses would have too much power and would inevitably cause dissension in the family of the Caesars.[160]

So the hatred of Agrippina for Tiberius grew, and Sejanus fuelled it by sending reports to her, under the guise of friendship, that Tiberius intended to poison her. One night at dinner when Tiberius offered her a piece of fruit, deliberately testing her because she had obviously not eaten, she revealed her suspicion by handing the fruit to a servant, and the angry, insulted Emperor never invited her to dine with him again. Once more Sejanus had succeeded. Rumours began to spread throughout the city that Tiberius planned to destroy his daughter-in-law, the granddaughter of Augustus.[161]

By this time, AD 26, Caligula was thirteen years old, and he lived with his mother. Although Tacitus does not tell us how he reacted to the machinations of Sejanus and Tiberius, we know that he was devoted to his family and must have been upset by the strong passions of Agrippina. Quite possibly his elder brothers, Nero and Drusus, realized the danger they were in and revealed their fear to the youngest of the princes. By age thirteen a young man begins to have a fairly strong political awareness – at least some young men do – but the sources do not tell us how Caligula reacted to the swirl of dynastic politics in the imperial capital.

Later in the same year Tiberius finally decided to leave Rome altogether. First he went to Campania, the great, fertile plain around Naples in southern Italy, and then to the beautiful Isle of Capri, a rocky, inaccessible retreat in the Bay of Naples. The ruins of his palace there still stand today. Although Sejanus had engineered this retirement from Rome, Tiberius was very fond of solitude. Earlier, during the reign of Augustus, he had left Rome for many years for the island of Rhodes. Tacitus claims that the Emperor wanted greater privacy for his lusts than he could get in the capital and also that old age had made him embarrassed at his appearance: 'He had indeed a tall, singularly slender and stooping figure, a bald head, a face full of eruptions, and covered here and there with plasters.'[162] Also, he wanted to get away from his ageing mother, who was becoming increasingly domineering.

Before the move from Campania to Capri Sejanus tightened his grip on the Emperor's loyalty even further by saving Tiberius' life during a rockfall at a cave entrance. While everyone else in the imperial party panicked, the Prefect remained calm, covered Tiberius' body with his own, and continued to protect the Emperor until military rescuers reached the scene. 'After this,' wrote Tacitus, 'Sejanus was greater than ever, and though his counsels were ruinous, he was listened to with confidence, as a man who had no care for himself.'[163]

If Tiberius' retirement to reclusive Capri also made Sejanus stronger, since he became the Emperor's representative in Rome, the official retinue joining the Emperor on the island suited the power-broker's purpose as well. It was a relatively harmless group politically. There was only one senator, Marcus Cocceius Nerva, grandfather of the future Emperor of the same name (Nerva, AD 96–8, the first of the 'five good emperors'). The Nerva of the Julio-Claudian period was a distinguished jurist, but probably not very active in the day-to-day affairs of the Roman Senate. In addition there was only one equestrian, Curtius Atticus. The imperial party consisted mainly of scholars, most of them Greek. At Rome soothsayers and astrologers had a field day when the Emperor departed. They predicted that he would never return, which proved to be true, but they had no idea that he would live on for eleven years.[164]

With Tiberius tucked safely away on Capri Sejanus decided to make his move against Agrippina and her sons. Late in 26 Nero, the eldest son of Germanicus, became Quaestor, the first office in the sequence of those held by politicians in Rome, thereby making him a full member of the Senate. This may have provoked Sejanus to action.[165] It is possible that Agrippina was put under house arrest at Herculaneum at this time and that Caligula was sent to live with the Emperor's mother, the octogenarian, Livia.[166] The Prefect arranged for charges to be brought against Nero, the eldest son of Germanicus. Nero was a modest young man, considering his station in life, but he was encouraged by his followers and former slaves to play the role of heir-designate more forcefully. The public and the army wanted a leader, Nero was told, and Sejanus would not dare to stand up to an imperial prince. According to Tacitus, Nero was not unusually ambitious, but he occasionally made thoughtless comments that spies reported with exaggeration. Since the reports were secret, the young Prince had no chance to defend himself. Soon Nero was in a hopeless position. People ignored or turned away from him. Sejanus' friends laughed at him. Tiberius seemed angry or treacherous. 'Whether the young Prince spoke or held his tongue, silence and speech were alike criminal.'[167]

Nero was married to Livia's daughter, and she reported all her husband's fears to her mother who was still Sejanus' lover. Finally Nero's brother Drusus turned against him, joining with Sejanus, who promised to support the younger brother for the throne. Drusus had a lust for power, a mean temper, and was envious because his mother Agrippina seemed to favour the elder brother. Then Sejanus used agents to advise Agrippina and Nero to flee to the Roman armies along the Rhine or to go to the Forum when it was crowded, embrace the statue of the divine Augustus, and appeal to the protection of the people and the Senate. When they refused to do these things, they were accused of having thought about doing them.[168]

This Thracian bust of the young Emperor Caligula reputedly shows the beard he grew while in mourning for his favourite sister, Drusilla, who died in the summer of AD 38. Caligula's grief became legendary, and Drusilla was the first Roman woman ever to be officially proclaimed a goddess.

(Right) Adopted son of Julius Caesar and the first Emperor of Rome, Augustus (27 BC–AD 14) developed a dynastic policy and laid the foundations of autocratic power – a power that later emperors, Caligula and Nero among them, were to abuse.

Augustus was almost as influential after his death: once deified, he was assiduously worshipped by his successors and the Roman people alike. (Right) Apotheosis in marble, Ravenna, c. AD 40. (Above) Bronze coin showing a ceremony in his temple – which was built under Tiberius and dedicated under Caligula.

(Below) The stern profile of
Marcus Agrippa, the powerful
general who was Augustus'
second-in-command. He married
the Emperor's daughter Julia in
AD 21, and their five children
included Caligula's mother,
Agrippina.

(Right) Portrait bust of the
Emperor Tiberius in old age.
Much of Caligula's adolescence
was spent witnessing the
promiscuity and erotic games of
Tiberius' notorious court on
Capri. Romans greeted the death
of Tiberius with joy, as heralding
(as they saw it) the end of an era
of tyranny and deprivation.

68

Caligula endeared himself to the populace during the early part of his reign by staging huge gladiatorial shows; but his apparent generosity soon revealed itself to be an obsession. According to Dio the Emperor required a daily performance of some kind. (Left) Relief showing a Roman chariot race. (Right) Bronze statuette of a Thracian gladiator. (Below left) Second-century mosaics, showing a bear trampling on a bestiarius and a mock-gladiatorial fight. Caligula once fought in a mock-contest against an opponent armed with a wooden sword – whom the Emperor then stabbed with a real dagger. (Below right) An orchestra plays for gladiators fighting: first-century mosaic.

Coins portraying (left) Livia as the personification of 'Salus' ('Health') and (right) Antonia. Both women – the first the imperious widow of Augustus and the second Caligula's grandmother – were responsible for the future Emperor's upbringing at different times. (Below) This coin showing Germanicus was struck by Caligula to honour his father after the death of Tiberius in AD 37. Tiberius had bitterly resented Germanicus' popularity and military achievements.

70

Bronze coin showing Caligula's three sisters – the eldest, Agrippina, mother of the future Emperor Nero; Drusilla; and Julia Livilla. According to Suetonius, Caligula committed incest with all three.

Caligula's elder brothers Nero and Drusus. Tiberius' ambitious minister Sejanus stirred up conflict between the two possible imperial heirs; Tiberius eventually sent Nero to the prison island of Pontia, and confined Drusus in the dungeon of the palace at Rome.

The first-century Grand Cameo of Paris or 'Gemma Tiberiana', possibly showing Tiberius receiving Germanicus on his return from the Rhine, or giving him his commission before his journey to the East. The figures behind Germanicus on the far left could be Agrippina and the five-year-old Caligula.

The year AD 27 witnessed another serious attack on the house of Germanicus. One of the most loyal friends of Agrippina and her sons, a high-ranking equestrian by the name of Titius Sabinus, who had publicly shown his support for Germanicus' family, was thrown into prison. A group of senators, eager to please Sejanus and secure high office for themselves, had conspired to destroy Sabinus and thereby discredit Agrippina, Nero and Drusus. One of them approached Sabinus, praised him for his continued support of a great Roman family, and spoke highly of Germanicus and Agrippina. Sabinus was taken in by this ruse and soon found himself complaining about Sejanus and even the Emperor.

The new-found friend then lured Sabinus into his house, and, while three other senators hid in the space between the roof and ceiling, Sabinus was again drawn into treasonous conversation. Immediately, he was accused by the cabal of informers. Tacitus reported this episode with outrage: 'Three Senators thrust themselves into the space between the roof and ceiling, a hiding-place as shameful as the treachery was execrable.'[169] At the urging of Tiberius in a letter that reached the Senate on 1 January AD 28, Sabinus was hauled off for execution and his body was thrown into the Tiber.

It was in this same year that Tiberius betrothed Caligula's sister, the Younger Agrippina, to Gnaeus Domitius Ahenobarbus. Nine years later, in the year Caligula became Emperor of Rome, Agrippina gave birth to the future Emperor Nero. In 29 Tiberius' mother Livia died. Emperor and mother had not been getting along very well in the years before her death; she was eighty-six when she died, and old age had made her even more imperious. For our story the death of Livia is of special interest because the funeral oration was delivered by the young Caligula, now seventeen years old, who had lived with her for the previous two years. The funeral was his first public appearance. Tiberius did not attend, and he delayed implementing his mother's will. Also he refused many of the honours that the Senate voted to her, including deification, claiming that they would go against her wishes. But, as Tacitus observed, the death of Livia was 'the beginning of an unmitigated and grinding despotism.'[170] The old woman had checked some of Tiberius' basest instincts. Now that she was gone, there were no constraints. Caligula was sent to live with his grandmother Antonia.

Almost immediately a letter from Tiberius was read in the Senate, one that may have been suppressed earlier by his mother. It was an attack on Agrippina and Nero. The Emperor accused his grandson of unnatural passions and a dissolute life. Agrippina was immune from accusations of moral misconduct – her reputation was too great. But Tiberius criticized her sharp tongue and her defiance. Tacitus reports that the Senate was panic-stricken and quiet, yet some unimportant members insisted on a debate. Still, leading senators did not know what to do, because Tiberius had merely levelled furious accusations and had not made it clear how the two should be dealt with. Crowds gathered about the Senate House, and people demonstrated, blessing the Emperor and claiming that the letter was a forgery. Attacks were made on Sejanus, and he then inflamed the Emperor, who demanded that the matter be turned over entirely to him. This the frightened Senate willingly did.

Unfortunately at this point Tacitus' narrative ends and the section dealing with the treatment of Agrippina and Nero is missing. From other sources, far less complete and reliable, it is possible to state that Nero was declared a public enemy and that he and his mother were removed in chains under heavy guard from Rome to prison islands off the coast of Italy. Nero was sent to Pontia and Agrippina to Pandateria where her mother Julia had also been confined. Agrippina was badly treated while imprisoned, and a centurion once beat her so severely that she lost an eye. When she attempted starvation, she was fed under force.[171]

In 30 Sejanus took the final step in removing his competitors for the throne. At the time Drusus was free and actually with Tiberius in Capri, but with the help of the Prince's wife, Sejanus brought charges against him, and the Senate also declared

Drusus a public enemy. He was imprisoned in the dungeon of the palace at Rome.[172] The fall of Drusus left only two possible heirs to imperial power, and they were both too young and inexperienced to assume office in the near future. They were Caligula, who had never been considered a likely candidate for the throne because of his two elder brothers, and the ten-year-old Tiberius Gemellus, Tiberius' grandson, the son of Drusus and Livia. Neither prince in 30 seemed an obstacle to the elevation of Sejanus.

Indeed, nothing stood in the way of Sejanus. He had reached a pinnacle of power nearly unparalleled for an equestrian – or for anyone outside the imperial family, for that matter. He was in many ways to Tiberius what Agrippa had been to Augustus. Sacrifices were offered to his statues, vows were made by his fortune, even his birthday was a public holiday. And finally Tiberius approved his engagement to Livia.[173] The climax came when the Emperor announced that he intended to become consul himself for the fifth time in the year 31 and that Sejanus would be his colleague in the office. Tiberius had been consul only twice during his own emperorship; once in 18 with Germanicus as his colleague and the other time in 21 with his son Drusus. Significantly on both occasions it was with his heir-designate. Was this his way of signifying that Sejanus would succeed him?

Whatever Tiberius may have planned for Sejanus, something happened in the year 31 to make the Emperor change his mind. Tiberius later claimed in his own brief autobiography, now lost but referred to by Suetonius, that he learned of Sejanus' scheming against the sons of Germanicus;[174] and we know from the Jewish historian Josephus that Tiberius' sister-in-law, Antonia, wrote a letter to him in Capri saying that Sejanus was plotting against him.[175] Antonia was highly respected in the imperial court and was possibly the only person Tiberius would have believed. Caligula had been living with her since the death of Livia, and she may have genuinely been concerned for his life.[176] Also from various sources we know that the official charge against Sejanus when he finally fell in the autumn of 31 was conspiracy against Tiberius and Caligula. Some time before that, in 31, the Emperor had summoned Caligula to Capri, probably for his protection and also possibly simply to keep an eye on him.

The fall of Sejanus is one of the most interesting stories in the annals of imperial Rome, and it has been carefully analysed by many historians of the last generation. Much confusion remains, but what follows is what I regard as the most likely explanation of the event and of the motives of the chief participants. Early in 31 Tiberius made Caligula a priest and indicated considerable respect for the young man.[177] It is true that Sejanus and his son were made priests at the same time, but Tiberius praised Caligula especially and indicated that he might succeed to the throne. Dio says that Sejanus might have moved immediately against Caligula, had the people not made such a show of support for him. The *plebs* still revered the memory of Germanicus and were delighted that his youngest son seemed to enjoy the imperial favour.[178]

Furthermore, Tiberius' treatment of Sejanus vacillated greatly. On some occasions he praised the Prefect lavishly and on others he criticized him. When Sejanus asked to come to Capri, Tiberius refused, saying that he planned to come to Rome soon.[179] Then the Emperor acted to reduce the honours paid to his minister. In this year, before Sejanus fell, Caligula's brother Nero was finally cruelly hounded to death. Why Tiberius allowed Sejanus to proceed in this instance is difficult to say, though the Emperor may have developed a strong dislike of Agrippina's eldest son. In any event, we are told that Nero committed suicide when an executioner approached him with a noose and with hooks for dragging his body to the Tiber. His body was cut to pieces and it was only with difficulty that any remains were retrieved later.[180]

Despite the continued success of Sejanus' persecution of Agrippina and her two eldest sons, the sudden emergence of Caligula as an imperial favourite alarmed the Prefect. He probably did begin to plot against the young Prince whom he had safely disregarded in earlier years. Tiberius, for his part, advanced carefully against him; Sejanus had become very strong in Rome, and the Emperor naturally moved against him cautiously and with some fear for his own safety. To disarm the potent minister, Tiberius let out word that he intended to give him Tribunician Power, the one remaining sign that Sejanus was marked for the succession.[181]

When the Emperor was finally ready to act, he did so with a sudden, deadly rapier thrust. He selected as his agent of destruction a man named Macro, whom he commissioned on Capri as his new Praetorian Prefect.[182] Macro went to Rome, entered the city at night (17 October AD 31), called on the consul Memmius Regulus and then the Prefect of the watchmen (*vigiles*), Publius Graecinius Laco, and informed them of the plan. On the morning of 18 October, Macro proceeded to a meeting of the Senate, told Sejanus in strictest confidence that he had come from Capri with the official announcement of Tribunician Power for the Praetorian Prefect, and accompanied the happy, smiling Sejanus into the Senate Chamber. There Macro approached the Praetorians who had been assigned as guards for the meeting, told them of his appointment as the new Prefect, and sent them back to camp with a promise of a bonus. Then he surrounded the temple where the Senate met with a detachment from the reliable watchmen (Macro had formerly been their commander), and delivered to the consuls the letter from Tiberius. One of the consuls, the more reliable one, had already been informed of the plot during the night. Macro did not even wait to hear the letter read, but instead he went directly to the camp of the Praetorians.[183]

The letter was long and rambling.[184] Sejanus sat for some minutes perplexed at what was happening, since there was much in it that seemed irrelevant as well as petty. But it soon became clear that Tiberius was informing the senators of his fear of Sejanus, and asking them to send one of the consuls with a military escort to him in Capri.[185] Finally he demanded that Sejanus be placed under arrest. Stunned by what had transpired,

77

Sejanus, surrounded by now hostile senators, who treated him with open abuse, slowly rose to meet his fate. Led off to prison, Sejanus was dejected, and he cringed in the face of his accusers.[186]

Crowds gathered in the streets. When the mighty fall, the news travels fast. People tore down Sejanus' statues and broke them to bits. They called for his execution. There was no sign that the Praetorians were going to attempt the rescue of their former commander, and on the same afternoon the Senate met again and imposed the death penalty on Sejanus. The execution was carried out immediately and the body was exposed to the abuse of the people for three days. Not much was left of it, but the few remains that could be assembled were thrown into the Tiber.[187]

It had all happened so quickly. In the morning Sejanus seemed destined to be named heir-designate, by evening he was dead and disgraced. Tiberius had struck from Capri like a bolt of lightning. He could not be sure, however, that his scheme would work, and he waited anxiously for news about it. He had assembled a flotilla to take him to the provincial armies if Sejanus succeeded in raising rebellion in Rome. Macro had been authorized, as a last resort, to release Drusus from his dungeon prison and proclaim him Emperor, but such an extreme measure proved unnecessary.

A few days later Sejanus' son was also executed. Then the former Prefect's wife, Apicata, wrote a letter to Tiberius revealing that Sejanus and Livia had killed his son Drusus. Apicata committed suicide, and Livia was starved to death by her own mother, the redoubtable Antonia. Sejanus had two other children, a young son and an even younger daughter, who were executed a couple of months later. The daughter was too young to know what was happening to her when she was led off to be raped by her executioner, since virgins could not be slain. The bodies of the brother and sister were exposed after the killings.[188]

The destruction of Sejanus came too late to save Germanicus' family, and it would be a mistake to assume that Tiberius' only complaints against Agrippina, Nero and Drusus were that they had displeased his adviser. It is possible that Sejanus did not even have to scheme against the Julians. Tiberius had his own reasons for hating Agrippina, and she had hers for hating him. Sejanus merely served as a willing agent in the destruction of the family. The Emperor in his autobiography was more than a little hypocritical in saying that Sejanus was destroyed because of his plots against the relatives of Germanicus. Although that may have seemed a convenient pretext, Suetonius was correct in remarking that Nero was not destroyed until after Tiberius had become suspicious of Sejanus, and that Drusus and Agrippina actually lived on after Sejanus' death.[189] On the other hand, it is also true that their destruction really came with their banishments, not with their executions, and they had all been driven into exile by Sejanus.

Still, Tiberius obviously loathed Agrippina and because of her had reason to suspect her two eldest sons. It was not long after the death of Sejanus that Drusus was starved in his dungeon prison. Tiberius sent a letter to the Senate and ordered the reading of a journal that had been kept for years of Drusus' comments about him, culminating in the furious remarks made during the period of starvation, when Drusus actually kept himself alive for several days by eating the stuffing of his mattress.[190] Shortly afterwards Agrippina died too, committing suicide by starvation. Tiberius wrote an even more remarkable letter on her death, saying that she was lucky she had not been strangled and exposed.[191] The age of Tiberius had become a period of depravity; a frightened Senate merely thanked Tiberius for the mercy he showed to Agrippina.

The ascendancy of Sejanus had a terrible effect on the young Caligula. The early years of the reign of Tiberius had been glorious ones for the young Prince, until he reached the age of seven when his father died under mysterious and tense circumstances in Syria. The boy had accompanied his grieving mother back to Rome and no doubt listened often to her passionate outbursts against the Emperor. For a while Tiberius restrained his resentment against the outspoken Princess, and her two older sons were treated with respect as the heirs-designate. But Agrippina's anger grew stronger as the rise of Sejanus threatened her family's position. Sejanus, enjoying for a long time the goodwill of the Emperor, played on the tension inherent in the dynasty and proved stronger than Agrippina and her sons, even though he was also eventually destroyed. Caligula was fortunate in his youth. Had he been older, he too would have fallen to the machinations of Sejanus.

4. *Caligula on Capri*

The young Caligula lived a life of turmoil. He was seven when his father died in the East, and then he lived for several years with his mother, brothers and sisters in a dangerous and highly emotional environment. At some point, possibly as early as the year 27, he left his mother's house to live with the ageing dowager Empress, Livia.[192] Life with Livia was unpleasant, and why Caligula went to her in the first place we do not know. Perhaps Tiberius ordered it, or Agrippina thought it best. In any event, the future Emperor was only about fifteen years old at the time and was seventeen when he gave Livia's funeral oration.

We know virtually nothing about Caligula's education. It was customary for upper-class Romans in the Julio-Claudian period to receive solid training in both Greek and Latin, and there is every reason to believe that the Prince was well educated, even though Suetonius says that literature was not one of his strong points.[193] He could quote Homer in Greek, and was a proud orator.[194] Undoubtedly he spent much time in study at this time of his life, though for his status in society he was probably only an average student with an above average ego. There is evidence that while still legally merely a child (*puer*) Caligula was designated an official in the government of some Spanish cities.[195]

After Livia's death began the brief period that was perhaps the happiest of his life. Caligula moved in with his grandmother, Antonia.[196] As we have seen, she was an extraordinary woman. Her father was none other than Mark Antony, the famous Triumvir and lover of Cleopatra, and her mother was Augustus' sister, Octavia. She was probably the most influential woman in the Roman Empire in the last years of the reign of Tiberius, and she seems to have inherited some of her father's connections with the eastern Mediterranean. She owned extensive properties in Egypt, had connections with Cleopatra's daughter, Cleopatra Selene (they were both daughters of Mark Antony) in Mauretania, and was a friend of the Herods of Judaea, especially M. Julius Agrippa, who lived at her house in Rome a few years before Caligula did.[197]

In the Acts of the Apostles (xii) this Julius Agrippa is called 'Herod Agrippa', though there is otherwise no evidence that he bore that name. Still, because the biblical reference has made the name so familiar, we shall refer to him as Herod Agrippa hereafter, and, in fact, he will play a reasonably important role in Caligula's life. The friendship was cemented later, but before Caligula became Emperor, and was undoubtedly enhanced by the mutual connection with Antonia.[198] Herod Agrippa was profligate, at least with money, and depended on the financial support of Antonia.

It is also likely that Caligula met the three sons of the Thracian king Cotys at Antonia's. There is an inscription from Cyzicus that describes them (Rhoemetalces, Polemo, and Cotys) as his 'companions'.[199] All three were given kingdoms of their own by Caligula after he became Emperor. Naturally there were other high-ranking Romans who frequented the house of Antonia, and Caligula's contacts there would have been numerous. As a son of Germanicus he was probably an object of attention and flattery. Drusilla and Livilla, two of Caligula's sisters, also stayed with Antonia during these years. Agrippina had married in 28.

Suetonius says that Caligula's incest with his sister Drusilla started in the three years they lived with Antonia (29–32).[200] The old lady is supposed to have found them in bed together. At this time Caligula would have been 17 to 20 years old, but Drusilla was only 14 to 17. The reports of Caligula's incest with all three of his sisters are far too firmly a part of the ancient record to be dismissed as lightly as they are by Balsdon, one of the major modern biographers of Caligula, when he says categorically,

'The charge of incest appears to be without foundation.'[201] It is difficult to fathom what Balsdon means by that, or what the French biographer Nony means when he attributes the incest, 'if it is true at all', to the curiosity of youth.[202] Likewise Barrett writes that 'the story need not be taken seriously'.[203]

Incest cannot be so easily dismissed, and it was as unacceptable in ancient Rome as it is today. Despite Balsdon and Barrett, there is no reason whatsoever to reject the ancient authors on this point. Caligula did commit incest with his sister Drusilla, and later on with the other two sisters as well. There is a story that, later, when Caligula was Emperor, he asked one of Rome's best-known wits, Passienus Crispus, whether he too had engaged in sex with his sister. 'Not yet', the tactful Passienus replied.[204] We shall return to this point eventually, because ultimately Caligula's sexual relations with his sisters had some political significance and entangled him in weird relations with their husbands and lovers.

While Caligula lived with Antonia, he began his official political career, at least after the fall of Agrippina and the two elder brothers. He became a priest (*pontifex*) at the same time as Sejanus and the latter's son, recommended by Tiberius in a letter that praised the young prince's loyalty.[205] The appointment of Caligula proved immensely popular with the people at Rome, and that made Sejanus jealous. As he planned to eliminate Caligula the way he had destroyed Agrippina, Drusus and Nero, Antonia sent her famous letter to Tiberius, and Sejanus fell. It was somewhat before that, in September or October of 31, that the Emperor summoned Caligula to Capri.[206]

Tiberius' life-style at Capri has been the subject of much attention. Moviegoers who saw the x-rated version of the *Penthouse* film on Caligula will perhaps remember those scenes in the palace at Capri as vividly as any, and anyone who has read Suetonius' *Lives of the Twelve Caesars* could scarcely forget the searing passages that describe the elderly Emperor's sexual deviations on the beautiful island.[207] Even today it is possible to visit the ruins of Tiberius' palace, and impossible not to imagine the activities reported to have gone on there by the scurrilous imperial biographer.

Tiberius had quite a reputation as a drinker and orgiast, even before he retired to Capri, and had appointed a Minister of Pleasures. But to the seclusion of that island the Emperor brought in young men and women from all over the Empire, skilled in the finest arts of sexual performance. Some rooms in the palace were decorated with pornographic scenes, sculpture, and erotic writings. Tiberius also hired young men and women to act as Pans and Nymphs in the woods nearby, so that he could see them engage in sex as he pleased. Soon the island became known as Caprineum, which means 'Goatland', a pun on the word Capri. We are told that he trained little boys – he called them his 'minnows' – to swim with him and to nibble between his legs. He also had babies who were still sucklings, for use in his baser moments. He was obviously more than the proverbial dirty old man; in his bedroom he had a painting of Atlanta performing fellatio on Meleager. Once he accosted two brothers after a religious ceremony, and when they complained about his behaviour, he had their legs broken.[208]

For the next five years Caligula lived with Tiberius on Capri, and the passion and anguish of his situation must have been nearly unbearable. He had loved his mother and brothers, yet on Capri he lived with one who hated Agrippina, and it was very important not to offend that man. To pretend not to be affected by the agonizing deaths of those members of his family may have been a greater strain than he could bear. The Freudian biographer, Hanns Sachs, believed that to be the case, and he may have been right, although it is more likely that the mental instability of Caligula went back even further, to his childhood and to the events surrounding the death of Germanicus. To what extent the sexual licence of the court on Capri twisted the future Emperor's mind is uncertain, but the environment can hardly be considered a normal one.[209]

Many modern historians believe that the stories of Suetonius and other ancient authors are the worst sort of gossip and rumour, and that they must be rejected as untrue. That was particularly so in the sexually naive and repressed period from 1850 to 1950, and it probably explains why Balsdon and others dismissed without qualms stories that were reported quite seriously by our sources from antiquity. But today it is possible to have a reasonably favourable view of Tiberius as Emperor and still believe that he was a sexual pervert. The selection of good governors and the building of roads need not be hampered by lust, and the vilest of men can be good administrators – not that Tiberius necessarily was. On the whole, the twentieth-century scholarly view of the Julio-Claudian Emperors has been much too favourable. They were a particularly sorry lot, road-building or no road-building. The excesses of modern scholarship in this regard are sometimes virtually staggering. Barrett writes that 'Caligula adopted an almost prudish attitude towards sex.'[210] It is one thing to be skeptical of rumour and innuendo in ancient authors, but quite another to throw out everything and turn their stories upside down.

The last years of Tiberius were painful ones, particularly for members of the dynasty and the senatorial aristocracy. After the fall of Sejanus Tiberius punished those who had supported the sinister deputy, yet many had done so only because the imperial minister seemed to be the Emperor's favourite. As a result, some were persecuted who did not deserve to be. One famous example is that of the equestrian, M. Terentius. He freely admitted that he had abetted Sejanus and had actively sought the minister's friendship. After all, Sejanus had nearly been a member of the imperial family, so why should an equestrian be hounded for supporting the regime? At least he thought that was what he was doing. For his courage in speaking out, Terentius was rewarded with an acquittal, although not many high-ranking Roman aristocrats fared so well.[211]

Again Caligula had to pretend not to be affected by the reign of terror, and perhaps he was not. Many things were happening in his own family, as Tiberius pulled the strings and made all the decisions. Shortly after arriving on Capri Caligula assumed the toga of manhood (*toga virilis*), although he was already much older than usual for that honour. Tiberius did not distribute money to the people on this occasion, although he had done so for Caligula's brothers.[212] Then the Emperor arranged a marriage for him with Junia Claudilla, the daughter of Marcus Junius Silanus, one of the consuls of 15 and a close friend of Tiberius. Silanus was a person of great integrity and distinction, and he was often asked first for his opinion in the Senate. Tiberius had such a high opinion of Silanus that he always refused to overturn any of his judicial decisions, and even to hear any appeals. The marriage was a good one for Caligula, and the Emperor attended the wedding in 35 at Antium. Unfortunately the young bride, Junia, died in childbirth the next year.[213]

Tiberius also arranged in 33 for the marriages of Caligula's sisters, Drusilla and Livilla.[214] Drusilla was betrothed to L. Cassius Longinus, consul of AD 30. This was not so good. Cassius was the grandson of the famous assassin of Julius Caesar. Although the grandson had been forgiven his lineage, the memory lived on. Only a few years before, Cremutius Cordus had been tried for praising Cassius as the last of the Romans, and, when the author committed suicide, his books were burned. Livilla married Marcus Vinicius, a prominent senator whose father had been a friend of Augustus and who himself eventually became a leading political figure in the reign of Claudius.[215] Earlier, in 28, Agrippina had married Gnaeus Domitius Ahenobarbus, who became consul in 32. Ahenobarbus was the grandson of Augustus' sister Octavia. Despite the impetuous temper and questionable morals of Ahenobarbus, Tiberius did not do badly for Caligula and his sisters.[216]

In these last years on Capri the question of the succession was on everyone's mind, including the Emperor's. There were really only three possible candidates – Caligula, his strange uncle Claudius (a family disgrace) and Tiberius Gemellus, the Emperor's grandson by Drusus. Claudius was out of the question. A physical cripple, he appeared foolish and had been kept in seclusion for years. Later, when he did become Emperor after Caligula's assassination, some thought he had merely pretended to be a fool. Others believed he really was a fool.[217] In any event, Tiberius never advanced him in politics and presumably never considered him seriously for the purple, despite Tacitus' claim that he did.[218]

Gemellus was still quite young. Born in AD 19, he was only about fifteen years old, and there were rumours that Tiberius' son Drusus was not his real father. The choices were unattractive, or worse, yet it was out of the question for Tiberius to consider anyone outside the Julio-Claudian family, as long as male heirs survived. The popularity of the Caesars still ran high, regardless of the present Emperor's reputation.[219]

Although the Emperor's health was failing, he pretended to be strong, simply to frustrate those who looked forward to his death. Naturally there were rumours of his impending demise. Augustus had banished the astrologers towards the end of his life, because they were predicting the inevitable.[220] In order to allay the unrest such portents caused, Augustus actually published his own horoscope. Belief in astrology was great in antiquity, though strict Roman pagans rejected it as atheistic since events were determined by the placement of the heavens, according to the astrologers, and not by the Roman gods. Often in the first century AD the Roman government banished the astrologers from the city (along with sorcerers, magicians, Jews, Christians, philosophers and other atheists – that is, people who did not believe in the Roman gods).[221]

On matters of this sort, however, Tiberius was different from the other emperors. He was a firm believer in astrology and had been, long before he became Emperor. When he was in exile on the island of Rhodes, he met the astrologer Thrasyllus, who eventually became an influential member of the court at Rome.[222] In fact, Thrasyllus' family had an amazing record in the capital. His son Balbillus was the court astrologer to the Emperors Claudius, Nero and Vespasian, and under Nero he served as Prefect of Egypt. Thrasyllus' granddaughter Ennia was married to the Praetorian Prefect Macro. Macro was so anxious to win the favour of Caligula, as it appeared that he would succeed Tiberius, that he encouraged his wife to have an affair with the still young prince, at least according to some ancient sources.[223] So the astrologer Thrasyllus had connections in the highest circles, and, not surprisingly, he kept predicting a longer life for the Emperor. According to one ancient source these forecasts saved the lives of many men, because Tiberius, who might have executed his enemies had he believed his end was near, let them live, thinking he had ample time to deal with them.[224]

The support of the Praetorian Prefect Macro was critical to the future of Caligula, and obviously also critical to the future of Macro himself. After replacing Sejanus, Macro grew very powerful – even if he was not quite as influential as his predecessor. Whereas Sejanus had actually aspired to the purple through a marriage alliance with the dynasty, Macro seems to have been content to be the power behind the throne. In the last years of Tiberius the best way to assure such power was to secure the favour of the Emperor's likely successor, and Macro made it clear that he supported Caligula. Tiberius even teased the Prefect about his obvious efforts to attach himself to the heir-designate, saying that he had turned his eyes 'from the setting to the rising sun';[225] and, as we have seen, Ennia, Macro's wife, seduced Caligula with the Prefect's blessing. The version in Philo and Suetonius, that the initiative was Caligula's and that Macro was ignorant of the affair, must be rejected in favour of the stories in Tacitus and Dio.[226]

In 33 Caligula held the quaestorship, the first political office in the sequence of offices that were customary for advancement in Rome. As Quaestor the future Emperor gained membership in the Senate, and Tiberius promised to promote him to the other offices five years earlier than usual. Although the Emperor was beginning to single out Germanicus' son for special favours, Caligula was not treated with the unusual attention that had been lavished on other potential heirs to the purple.[227] Under Augustus, Tiberius had been entrusted with delicate assignments from an early age. When he was twenty, in 23 BC, he prosecuted conspirators against the regime, and in 20 BC he went east on a major military expedition that took him into Armenia, where he actually crowned a new king on Rome's behalf and negotiated a settlement with the Parthians. Later, Augustus also used his grandsons, Gaius and Lucius, in responsible positions at an early age. They were even permitted to serve as consuls when they were twenty. After their deaths, in the period from AD 4–14, the last years of Augustus, Tiberius' sons, Germanicus (by adoption) and Drusus, were also treated in extraordinary fashion.[228]

In fact, Augustus and Tiberius had both handled earlier potential heirs with far greater respect than Caligula received. The point is important because it involves more than respect. Previous possible heirs were also given responsible commands that would have helped prepare them to assume the imperial throne. Tiberius, his brother Drusus, Gaius and Lucius Caesar, Germanicus, and Tiberius' son Drusus all served apprentice-ships. Had they actually ascended to the purple, they would have been prepared for it, as Tiberius was. Caligula never got this training.

It is not difficult to explain why the Emperor refused to use Caligula and his grandson Tiberius Gemellus in significant roles. After the death of Sejanus he was afraid to trust them. Caligula had to be kept on a tight leash at Capri, though he probably spent some time in Rome even in these years. It was during his year as Quaestor in AD 33 that his imprisoned brother and his banished mother died. Caligula had no recourse but to show his loyalty to the Emperor, yet it certainly caused him severe internal tension.

After the death of Agrippina her enemy Plancina, wife of Piso, was driven to suicide by new charges against her. Possibly Caligula was responsible for bringing down his mother's foe, but there is no evidence.[229] Tiberius had not liked Plancina but had spared her for his mother, Livia's, sake, albeit grudgingly. Then after the death of the dowager Empress in 29, the Emperor let Plancina live on, simply to taunt and humiliate Agrippina. But when Agrippina committed suicide, and her son Caligula seemed the obvious candidate for the succession, there was no longer any reason to protect one who had been such a notorious enemy of the house of Germanicus.

The popularity of Germanicus' family can be illustrated by an event of the year 34, the appearance in the East of a false Drusus Caesar. According to Dio, in Greece and Asia 'the cities received him gladly and espoused his cause.'[230] Eventually, however, the pretender was arrested. It is amazing how many false Caesars arose in the Early Roman Empire, claiming to be fallen members of the imperial family. Earlier there had been a false Agrippa Postumus, and later a false Nero would appear. The house of Caesar and Augustus had a vast following throughout the Roman world. It is all the more remarkable when many of the genuine Caesars were such abysmal creatures. Neither Agrippa Postumus, Drusus Caesar, nor Nero were exactly the most admirable members of the dynasty.

In these last years of Tiberius on Capri, Caligula experienced many strong feelings, and undoubtedly some of them contributed to his mental instability. He was openly accused of homosexuality and profligacy, probably with just cause.[231] His family life was an unmitigated catastrophe. The deaths of his mother and brother were compounded by the tragic death in childbirth of his wife Junia after only one year of marriage. It is likely that after that he began his affair with Macro's wife, Ennia.[232] Insofar as his personal relationship with Tiberius is concerned, the young prince was careful to please him in every respect. He obsequiously followed all of Tiberius' moods: one wag later wrote, 'There has never been a better slave or a worse master.'[233] Yet his love for the members of his immediate family must have caused incredible anguish.

In any event, it all mercifully came to an end when Tiberius died in 37 at Misenum on the Bay of Naples. The news of the Emperor's death provoked joy and celebrations in Rome. The people were tired of their stingy ruler and looked forward to the pleasures of government under the young son of the popular Germanicus. He offered them a new life, a gayer, happier time, a future of unrestrained joy combined with imperial grandeur. Life under Caligula promised youthful exuberance and continued sway over all the world. The good times had come.

People believed this, despite ugly rumours about how Tiberius had died. The day was 16 March AD 37. The Emperor had fallen seriously ill and was unconscious. But then he seemed to make a remarkable recovery. Some sources say that when he asked for the signet ring that had been removed from his finger, Macro and Caligula smothered him with his own bedclothes. In some versions only Macro and in others only Caligula was involved. Another version states that he tried to get out of bed and fell down dead, all on his own. The fact is that we shall never know for certain how he died, but Romans generally were happy to hear the news. Crowds gathered shouting 'Tiberius to the Tiber', hoping that the hated Emperor would be denied a decent funeral.[234]

Caligula refused to satisfy the mob in that way. He arranged for the body to be transported to Rome in much the same manner as Augustus' had been, with a military escort. It arrived in the city on 29 March. Caligula asked that his predecessor be deified, but the Senate refused, and the new Emperor did not press the point. Romans prepared for the dawning of a new age, and on 3 April Caligula himself delivered the funeral oration.[235]

But the accession of the new Emperor was not without its ambiguities. Tiberius had managed, even in his death, to obfuscate the situation: he had made a will in 35 in which he left Caligula and Tiberius Gemellus his equal, joint heirs. Ancient sources are filled with statements that Tiberius did not trust or respect Caligula, yet he could not have set the son of Germanicus aside in favour of his other grandson, who was only a teenager. Although the old Emperor supposedly once told Caligula that he had all the bad elements of Sulla's character and none of the good, and declared that the Prince was a danger to the ruler and to the public, he had a strange tolerance for the young man.[236] Suetonius suggests that Tiberius hoped to soften the 'savage nature' of Caligula by indulging his weaknesses.[237] The older man could not bring himself to leave the popular youth in uncontested sovereignty, however, but in dividing his property Tiberius sealed the fate of his younger grandson, Tiberius Gemellus, who was later killed. Despite the arguments of the two biographers Balsdon and Barrett, there is no reason to believe that Tiberius saw any real merit in the son of Germanicus. The sources make it clear that the young man simply bent over backwards to avoid giving the Emperor any pretext for eliminating him.

In making Caligula and Tiberius Gemellus joint heirs to his property, the late Emperor had created a crisis, perhaps intentionally. Tiberius had not specifically named the heirs to his property joint heirs to the throne of imperial Rome, but there was no law of succession, and it was probably natural to assume that the heirs to the estate were also intended to be the inheritors of the purple.[238] There is no doubt that everyone found the will an embarrassment.

With the eager support and advice of Macro, Caligula moved quickly to seize power. Even while Tiberius was still alive, on his deathbed, the Praetorian Prefect had sent agents to the provincial governors and to the legions, some of which were stationed at points weeks distant from Rome, so that they might immediately proclaim Caligula Emperor. As soon as Tiberius died on 16 March, Macro administered the oath of allegiance to the troops and fleet in the Bay of Naples. Quickly he informed the consuls at Rome, and on 18 March the Senate met to take the oath to the new Emperor. At that time no one yet knew of the contents of the will Tiberius had written in the year 35. The Senate sent representatives to congratulate Caligula in person, and the equestrians sent a delegation headed by the Emperor's uncle, Claudius. A few days after the slow funeral cortège reached Rome on 29 March, the Senate met, and Macro read the will. Although it contained some popular provisions granting gifts to citizens and soldiers, the main terms, making Caligula and Tiberius Gemellus joint heirs, met stiff resistance. As a result the Senate declared the will null and void, taking the groundless position that Tiberius had been mentally incompetent when he made it.[239]

Caligula announced that he would pay the bequests to the people and the army anyway. The Roman Senate and people had shown their loyalty to the new ruler; he would repay them many times over, in ways they never imagined.

5. The Highest Hopes

The accession of Caligula, according to Suetonius, 'fulfilled the highest hopes of the Roman people, of all mankind.'[240] The son of Germanicus had escaped the schemes of Sejanus and the suspicions of Tiberius. With the help of Macro and Antonia the new Emperor began his reign under the most favourable conditions. In the first three months over 160,000 animals, sacrificial victims, were slain in the temples in celebration of Caligula's accession.[241] The Senate on 28 March AD 37, conferred all the imperial powers upon the new Emperor, but Caligula refused to accept the title of *Pater Patriae*, Father of his Country, and to use the title *Imperator* as his first name.[242] Before his accession his full legal name had been Gaius Julius Caesar Germanicus. On 28 March he became Gaius Caesar Augustus Germanicus. In his inaugural speech to the Senate, the twenty-four-year-old Emperor promised deferential cooperation and respect, saying that he was the son and ward of the Senate.[243] Altogether there was a nearly frenzied reaction by Romans to the change in their political environment.

Everything had been done quickly, and the constitutional details of Caligula's assumption of power were not immediately known throughout the Empire. There is an interesting inscription from Aritium in Lusitania, revealing the nature of the oaths and the constitutional uncertainty:

Gaius Ummidius Durmius Quadratus being the propraetorian legate of Gaius Caesar Germanicus, imperator.
Oath of the Aritians.
On my conscience I will be the enemy of those whom I find to be the

enemies of Gaius Caesar Germanicus and if anyone threatens or shall threaten danger to him and his safety I will not desist from the pursuit of him until he has paid the penalty to Caesar in full; and I will not hold myself or my children dearer than his safety and I will regard those who may have a hostile attitude towards him as my enemies. If I am deliberately acting falsely, now or in the future, then may Jupiter Optimus Maximus and divine Augustus and all the other immortal gods deprive me of my country, my safety and all my fortunes.[244]

This oath was taken on 11 May, fifty-two days after the death of Tiberius, and the new Emperor is referred to as *Imperator*, but not as *Augustus*. Out in the provinces some of the constitutional niceties could simply be ignored. It is likely that the Senate in Rome voted full power to Caligula on 28 March, the first day he arrived in the city. Suetonius writes: 'When he entered the city, full and absolute power was at once put into his hands by the unanimous consent of the Senate and the mob, which forced its way into the House. . . .'[245] The powers it had taken Augustus a lifetime to accumulate, Caligula received in a single moment. The text of the senatorial decree has not survived, but it must have been similar to the one that does survive from the accession of Vespasian in AD 69, the so-called *Lex de Imperio Vespasiani*.[246]

Although quite young to rule the Roman Empire, at twenty-four Caligula was a fully grown adult, and we have descriptions of him in ancient sources.[247] He was big and tall, with a thin neck and thin legs. He had hollow eyes and temples, a broad forehead, and thin hair, balding on top, although his body was hairy. His complexion was pale, and he had large feet. Seneca and Suetonius agree that he was ugly. The coins of his reign show him not to have been grotesque in appearance, however. As one modern biographer puts it, he lacked '. . . the refined delicacy of Augustus' image, but also the squat ugliness of Nero's. The most noticeable and consistent features are the elongated forehead (confirming Suetonius), a somewhat bulbous nose, a slightly pointed chin, and a mouth with a retracted lower lip.'[248] Temperamental and quarrelsome, he also suffered from insomnia. Suetonius says that as a boy he experienced epilepsy, but from the description of his symptoms it seems to have been the *petit mal* rather than the *grand mal* variety.[249]

In his funeral oration over the body of Tiberius he had shed many tears; yet he said little about the dead Emperor and devoted most of his comments to Augustus and Germanicus.[250] The Senate actually refused to deify Tiberius although Caligula proposed it, but there was a suspicion that he asked merely as a formality.[251] He did not attend the meeting when the matter was discussed, and after the Senate refused to act on the request, he never brought it up again, confirming the instincts of the senators.[252]

One of the Emperor's most popular acts was a pilgrimage he made at the outset of his reign to the islands where his mother and brother had died in exile.[253] There was considerable pity among the Romans for the suffering of his family, and when he went to gather the ashes of his loved ones, his subjects opened their hearts in sympathy and adoration. Caligula made a show of the undertaking. After crossing over the sea in stormy weather, he personally placed their ashes in urns and sailed with them in a bannered bireme to Ostia at the mouth of the Tiber and then up the river to Rome. The most distinguished equestrians were selected to carry the urns to the mausoleum of Augustus. The urns have actually survived into the twentieth century.[254] It is uncertain whether the remains of his brother Drusus, who had died in prison, were ever discovered, but his memory was commemorated as well.[255] The whole affair was turned into a kind of parade, similar to a Roman triumph. He also rescinded all measures that had been voted against his family and released from banishment those Romans who had been persecuted for their support of the household of Germanicus.[256] A coin was minted in honour of Nero and Drusus, and their statues were displayed in Rome.[257]

Caligula proposed additional honours for his mother and father. The month of September was renamed Germanicus although there is no evidence that the new name was ever used.

He decreed funeral sacrifices each year for his mother Agrippina and games in the Circus, her image being transported in a carriage during the procession. Coins were minted in her honour celebrating the occasion of the games.[258] Although dead members of the imperial family had been commemorated in various ways in the past, and in fact honours had been paid by Tiberius to the memory of Germanicus, this is the first occasion in the imperial period when individuals who had been condemned by the Senate were resurrected in this way. The intricacies of dynastic politics were beginning to unfold.

For his living relatives Caligula sponsored even greater recognition. His sisters, Drusilla, Livilla, and Agrippina, were made honorary Vestal Virgins, though the 'honorary' designation did not, fortunately, convey any requirement for chastity.[259] These distinctions for young women were unprecedented. They were included in the oaths taken to the Emperor: 'I shall not hold myself or my children dearer than I do Gaius [Caligula] and his sisters.'[260] The consuls began their motions in the Senate with the statement, 'Favour and good luck to Gaius and his sisters.' Their images appeared on coins as 'Security', 'Peace', and 'Prosperity' (*Securitas, Concordia, Fortuna*).[261]

The elderly Antonia also received extraordinary honours. She was given the title Augusta by the Senate, as Livia had been, although Suetonius says that she declined to use it during her lifetime.[262] Even Caligula's uncle Claudius received the public recognition that had been denied under Augustus and Tiberius. Although Caligula had declined the offer of one of the two consuls to resign so the Emperor could take his place, he did agree to be elected substitute consul later in the same year, with Claudius as his colleague in office.[263] The elevation of Claudius shows how deeply Caligula felt about the humiliation and suffering of his family, for if the truth be known, there had been good reason to keep Claudius in the closet. Despite modern scholarly arguments and Robert Graves' novels, the real Claudius was a bumbling embarrassment to the dynasty. Yet, the Emperor's devotion to family was popular with the Roman people.[264]

97

Finally, he won even more approval by the way he treated his competitor for the throne, Tiberius Gemellus. Caligula adopted the young man, let him assume the toga of manhood, and appointed him the 'Prince of Youth' (*Princeps Iuventutis*), a title that Augustus had given his grandsons, Gaius and Lucius Caesar.[265] This effectively made Tiberius Gemellus heir-designate, although the new, twenty-four-year-old Emperor might be expected to stay in office for a long time to come. Still, it appeared to be a generous gesture on the part of Caligula, who could perhaps yet have a male heir of his own.

One of Caligula's first acts as Emperor was to free all prisoners, granting amnesty to exiles everywhere.[266] This, too, was immensely popular, since most Romans believed that political prisoners had been victims of the tyranny of Tiberius. Furthermore, Caligula allowed all writings that had earlier been banned to recirculate freely. He also publicly destroyed all records of the cases involving members of his family, burning the files and letters in the Forum, and claimed that he had not read any of them and that no one who had accused them need fear retribution. Finally, he announced that there would be no more treason trials; the tyranny of Tiberius had ended. There seemed to be an atmosphere of openness under the new ruler, who did not suffer from the suspicions and sensitivities of his predecessor.[267]

To win the favour of the Praetorian Guard and the people Caligula dispersed large sums of money. Tiberius had willed one thousand sesterces to each member of the Guard, but Caligula paid twice that amount, despite the revocation of the will. To every citizen on the grain dole the Emperor paid the sum decreed by Tiberius and an additional three hundred sesterces. That was on 1 June AD 37. About fifty days later, on 19 July, he gave them another three hundred.[268] In the days of Cicero the annual subsistence income for a family of four was about one thousand sesterces, so these monetary gifts were substantial.[269] In fact, Caligula also paid out the sums bequeathed by Livia, since Tiberius had never done so. Equally important, as far as the *plebs* were concerned, was the fact that Caligula renewed the games on a lavish scale. In an effort to save money Tiberius had drastically curtailed them, and Romans had regarded him as stingy. Caligula seemed to please everyone.[270]

Nor did he neglect the Senate. On his accession he had promised to treat senators with respect. When he assumed the consulship with Claudius on 1 July, he reiterated that promise and scathingly denounced Tiberius for the crimes of his reign. The Senate was so impressed with this speech that it decreed that it should be read every year.[271] He dedicated the temple of the divine Augustus which had been under construction throughout the reign of Tiberius. It was an occasion for wining and dining members of the Senate and their families and for offering great pageants to the Roman people. As part of the ceremony four hundred bears and four hundred Libyan lions were slain amid much horse-racing and other games. Although Caligula served as consul for only two months, from 1 July to 31 August AD 37, before he and Claudius resigned the office in favour of others, he used his tenure in office as an opportunity for entertaining all orders of Roman society.[272]

There was only one stain on the otherwise happy record of the first few months of the new regime. Antonia died on 1 May after quarrelling with the new Emperor. Suetonius says that Caligula refused her a private audience, insisting that Macro be present at their meeting, and that by this and similar irritations he caused her death. Ominously the biographer adds, 'Some think that he also gave her poison.'[273] Dio Cassius claims that the Emperor drove his grandmother to suicide because she had chastized him for something. He is reported to have told her, 'Remember, I have the right to do anything to anybody.'[274] He apparently paid her no special honour on her death and merely watched her burning funeral pyre from his dining room. It is likely, however, that whatever problem existed between the two of them, if there is any truth to the tradition, it was kept within the palace and did not become a cause for gossip in the city generally.

Not long after stepping down from the consulship Caligula

fell seriously ill and nearly died.[275] As he recovered, he began to show the signs of the tyranny for which he became notorious. Some scholars have argued that it was this illness that made him mad. Before we look carefully at the nature of his disease, it is necessary to examine the record of the first six months of his reign to determine whether it shows any signs of the instability that characterized the rest of the reign. We have already seen that as a teenager and young adult Caligula suffered severely from the mistreatment of his family by Sejanus and Tiberius. The anguish was intensified by the need to pretend that it did not matter, that the punishment meted out to his mother and brothers was actually justified.

We must ask ourselves whether his experiences, say from the time of his father's death, when Caligula was only seven, to the moment of his accession, might in themselves have caused him mental instability, and the answer is obviously yes.[276] It is also possible that he had a genetic disorder and was somewhat unbalanced from the beginning. In other words, if we can find some indication of erratic behaviour before his illness late in 37, we need not attribute his later, obvious madness to whatever disease he suffered in that year, although the ailment may have contributed to a previously existing disorder.

We should set aside, at least for the moment, the allegations about Caligula's role in the death of Antonia. They may have been based on unfounded rumour, and superficially at least they seem inconsistent with the rest of the evidence suggesting that the first few months of the reign were happy. But there are at least two other indications of instability – profligacy with money and an inordinate fascination with the games, the circus and the theatre.

It is true that Tiberius had left a vast surplus in the treasury when he died.[277] He had been a miser, and his parsimonious policies had probably led to a shortage in the money supply later in his reign.[278] The central government simply did not put enough coins into circulation, because it was not spending enough. The annual budget of the Roman Empire in the second century AD has been estimated at about eight hundred million sesterces.[279] In the time of Augustus and Tiberius it was probably about half that, though possibly somewhat more. Tiberius had left a surplus of two thousand seven hundred million which would be roughly five to six years' revenue.[280] Caligula spent it all in less than one year, and that reckless expenditure began in those first few months.[281] One of the first things the new Emperor did was to publish the imperial budget, suggesting an openness in financial affairs that Tiberius had not shown, but Caligula probably never repeated the gesture.[282] Obviously extravagant expenditure after the restrictive policies of Tiberius would have seemed wonderful to most Romans, and it was reasonable for a new Emperor to modify fiscal policy and spend money at a somewhat greater rate. Yet Caligula did go beyond the bounds of fiscal responsibility.

Early in his reign, for example, he awarded a freed woman (a former slave) eight hundred thousand sesterces because she had not informed on a crime committed by her former owner, even though she had been subjected to torture.[283] Ostensibly this may seem a generous gesture and undoubtedly did to Romans at the time. However, it was more than generous; it was extravagant. It was twice the amount required for equestrian status in Rome and very near the one million sesterces set as the base for membership of the senatorial order.

More dramatically, Caligula restored some kings who had been deposed by Tiberius to their thrones and awarded them all the arrears of revenue that had accumulated during the interval. Antiochus of Commagene received a hundred million sesterces,[284] and that was in addition to the return of his territory which had been organized as a Roman province. A hundred million sesterces was about twenty-five per cent of the annual revenues of the Roman Empire, and was a settlement wildly out of line with anything that could be considered reasonable. Seneca reported that Caligula once spent ten million sesterces on a single dinner, an amount equal to the tribute of three provinces, and the philosopher and politician added that Nature had created Caligula merely to show 'how far supreme vice, when combined with supreme power, could go. . . .'[285]

As for the games and the theatre, which were also quite costly, Caligula, to be sure, had legitimate reason for celebration in the first few months of his reign. Again, it was reasonable that he fund them lavishly, considering popular discontent with the behaviour of Tiberius. But later he became famous for his excesses in the games and the theatre, and his activities in the first six months of his reign did show the signs of that vice.[286]

Tiberius had actually opposed the games and theatrical performances for several reasons. They were considered immoral by some Romans because they attracted a bad crowd.[287] Augustus had regulated them carefully, and Tiberius, who was an enemy of public *levitas* (one of his critics might translate that as 'having fun'), imposed additional restrictions.[288] He discouraged attempts to create new games in his honour, reduced and strictly controlled the cost, and banished senators or equestrians who performed on stage or in the arena. He even exiled some actors and theatregoers from Rome.[289]

Caligula reversed this policy.[290] Initially his attitude was popular, but in time it became one of the chief grievances against him. He simply went too far.[291] The fascination that sports figures and actors have for leaders of state is well known – the late President Kennedy is famous for his association with them – yet even today, actors and actresses have a somewhat salacious reputation, and that was true in antiquity. Caligula showed no restraint in his desire for their company and in his infatuation with them as a class. The public spectacles became an obsession for the Emperor. Suetonius says that already on Capri Caligula was addicted to the theatrical arts of singing and dancing.[292] When Claudius came to the throne, he reintroduced the restrictions that had prevailed previously, indicating that Caligula's policies had become scandalous.[293] The new Caesar had a homosexual relationship with the famous actor Mnester, and another actor, Apelles, was always close to him, and on at least one occasion even became involved in a matter of state.[294]

The Emperor's preoccupation with the games and the theatre revealed itself at least from the onset of his reign, if not earlier. Huge sums were spent from the very beginning. According to Dio, Caligula required some kind of performance every day.[295] It is possible that the Emperor's sycophants in the Senate proposed games willy-nilly in the ruler's honour and that Caligula happily went along. Indeed, he was anxious to have large crowds, and in order to attract them he suspended mourning and postponed lawsuits.[296] He reversed a decree of Tiberius and permitted people to come to the games barefoot.[297] The games for the dedication of the temple of Augustus involved two days of horse-racing with twenty races on the first day and forty on the second.[298] The pay of actors, gladiators, charioteers and other performers was the obligation of the government or of the officials responsible for organizing the performances. In any event the cost was high, and Tiberius had tried to control it. Caligula went far beyond even the pre-Tiberian precedents.[299]

There is ample evidence that even in the early months of the new regime, happy though they were, the young Caesar embarked on a ruinous fiscal policy. Under the influence of Macro, Caligula made no serious errors in the treatment of Senate and *plebs*. He said all the right things and was able briefly to conceal the many hatreds and frustrations that seethed beneath the surface. According to Philo, Macro watched carefully over the young Caesar, waking him up when he fell asleep at banquets, and restraining him when he enjoyed dirty jokes too obviously or tried to join in dancing that excited him. Always Macro urged the Emperor to maintain his dignity. Macro even controlled Caligula's daily agenda, screening the people who sought a private meeting.[300] But Caligula approached the celebrations with wild abandon, and the torments of his earlier life would soon be revealed. The months from March to October of 37 do not make Caligula an untroubled youth. With the benefit of sage advice and the goodwill of all the world it is not surprising that he had an initial brief 'honeymoon'. In the end it proved brief indeed.

So it is clear that Caligula's illness in September and October was not the cause of his mental problems, although it might easily have made them worse. It seems to have been a dangerous disease, from which the Emperor suffered.[301] All over the Empire there was concern. Crowds gathered to hear the latest news. It is not possible today to know with certainty what ailment the Emperor had, but some believe it was a nervous breakdown caused by the excitement of the first few months of the reign. Others have proposed such possibilities as encephalitis, hyperthyroidism, a virus affecting the central nervous system, and the effects of epilepsy. The vagueness of ancient authors permits many possibilities, but, as we have seen, Caligula's mental problems had their origins in his earlier experiences, and they were not the result of his sickness in 37.

6. *From Joy to Terror*

It was not long before Caligula revealed to his contemporaries some weird interests and traits of personality. After the Emperor recovered from his illness, he heard that the frenzy of concern for his health which had swept through Rome had induced two citizens to make unusual vows.[302] One, Publius Afranius Potitus, had sworn that he would sacrifice his own life for the Emperor's recovery. Caligula made him do so, and actually staged the death as a public event, turning the man over to slaves who were ordered to parade him through the streets with sacrificial decorations and hurl him off an embankment (possibly the Tarpeian rock). Another, Atanius Secundus, a wealthy equestrian, had vowed to fight a gladiator, and the Emperor not only forced him to do just that but insisted, despite the man's pleas, that he fight on until he won.[303]

After recovering from his illness Caligula began to strike out wildly against some of the most prominent members of his court. In quick succession he killed or drove to suicide his adopted son and heir-designate, Tiberius Gemellus, his father-in-law, Marcus Junius Silanus, and his Praetorian Prefect and chief adviser, Macro. At least one biographer believes that they may have conspired against the Emperor as he apparently lay dying, but there is no ancient evidence to support the view.[304] It is far more likely that Gemellus, Silanus, and Macro took the government into their own hands while Caligula was incapacitated, and that he resented their influence as he began to recover.

In any event, some time in the winter of AD 37/38 Caligula required his father-in-law, the distinguished senator, M. Junius Silanus, to commit suicide. The senator's daughter, Junia

Claudilla, had died the year before, while she and Caligula were on Capri with Tiberius. Silanus took advantage of his position as the Emperor's father-in-law to give unwanted advice, treating the Prince as his own son. His crime was that, claiming seasickness, he had not gone to sea when the Emperor had. Caligula accused him of wanting the throne and hoping for a shipwreck.[305] After considerable humiliation Silanus slit his own throat.

Even more sinister was the demise of the young Tiberius Gemellus, grandson of Tiberius. Caligula charged him with having prayed for the Emperor's death. Apparently Gemellus drank a cough medicine that Caligula, smelling it on the young man's breath, mistook for an antidote for poison. Gemellus, when accused, offered a famous reply: 'An antidote – how can one take an antidote against Caesar?'[306] Caligula simply sent a military tribune to execute Gemellus without warning.[307] His gravestone has survived, probably from the mausoleum of Augustus.[308]

Then, in the spring of 38, the Emperor turned against his chief supporters in the court, the Praetorian Prefect, Macro, and his wife, Ennia.[309] Macro had skilfully engineered Caligula's accession and, according to some, had presided over the death of Tiberius, helping the ageing Emperor leave the world without crisis. Ennia had become Caligula's lover. In the beginning the new Emperor had worked closely with Macro and continued his relationship with Ennia. He even rewarded his faithful servant with an appointment as Prefect of Egypt, a position Macro did not live to enjoy.[310] Apparently Macro presumed to give his protégé advice on government, a reasonable thing for the Prefect to do, considering his role in arranging the transferral of power to the new Emperor. A recent biographer compares this with William II of Germany 'tiring of his Bismarck', but neglects to mention that William did not find it necessary to kill Bismarck.[311]

Philo the Jew, a contemporary witness to the events of the regime and an invaluable source, writes that the Emperor tired quickly of Macro's personal style and influence. Apparently Caligula began to say to bystanders, as Macro approached him:

Here comes the teacher of one who no longer needs to learn, the tutor of one who is no longer in tutelage, the censor of his superior in wisdom, who holds that an emperor should obey his subjects, who rates himself as versed in the art of government and an instructor therein, though in what school he has learnt its principles I do not know. For I from the cradle have had a host of teachers, father, brothers, uncles, cousins, grandparents, ancestors, right up to the founders of the House, all my kinsmen by blood on both the maternal and paternal sides, who attained to offices of independent authority, apart from the fact that in the original seeds of their begetting kinglike potentialities for government were contained. . . . And then does anyone dare to teach me, who even while in the womb, that workshop of nature, was modelled as an emperor, ignorance, dare to instruct knowledge?[312]

Adding insult to injury, Caligula also accused Macro of being a pimp for his wife.[313] Balsdon has compared the fall of Macro with the fall of Sejanus, saying that Macro suffered from 'his own presumption', but there is no evidence that Macro hoped to secure the throne for himself, and the comparison is odious: Macro was not a scheming murderer.[314] To prevent the accumulation of power by one man, Caligula appointed two new Praetorian Prefects.[315]

There is no reason to believe that the deaths of these prominent people significantly diminished the popularity of the Emperor. Romans were still prepared to make excuses for their young ruler. It was said that Silanus made a fool of himself and that Macro had too much pride and had not followed the Delphic rule, 'Know Thyself'. The reaction to Gemellus' death was that there cannot be two men running the government. Competition between two princes lead to factions, and factions lead to civil war. The goodwill Caligula had inherited from his father Germanicus also buffered him from criticism in the early part of his reign.[316]

Another incident at about this time revealed the capricious temperament of the young Emperor. A prominent member of the senatorial aristocracy, C. Calpurnius Piso, later the leader of the famous Pisonian conspiracy against Nero, had arranged to marry Livia Orestilla. Caligula attended the ceremony and ordered the bride to be taken to his own house. According to one version of the story, the Emperor, reclining on a couch next to Piso at the wedding banquet, sent him a note saying, 'Don't make love to my wife', whereupon he whisked the bride away from the feast and issued a proclamation the following day that he had taken a wife in the style of Romulus and Augustus, referring to the rape of the Sabine women and Augustus' affair with Livia while she was married to her previous husband. Caligula's marriage to Orestilla lasted only a few days before he divorced her.[317]

At some point during his reign Caligula did make one change in imperial policy that was both popular and sound. The sons of senators had been permitted by Augustus to wear the *latus clavus*, the toga with the broad purple stripe that singled them out as members of the senatorial aristocracy. According to Dio, in a passage that has been hotly debated by modern scholars, Caligula permitted the sons of equestrians to wear the *latus clavus* also, if they were deemed suitable for a senatorial career. Constitutionally this had the effect of making the senatorial order hereditary. In practice it always had been largely so, but under Caligula it became a legally closed order, open only to the sons of senators and to equestrians especially selected for membership by the Emperor. The sons of newly created senators automatically qualified for the *latus clavus*.[318]

After the deaths of Tiberius Gemellus and Macro, the Emperor's sisters moved into the spotlight of dynastic intrigue. Claudius was considered a laughing-stock, despite having held the consulship with Caligula. At the games the people were always glad to see him and shouted out 'Good luck to the emperor's uncle', or 'Good luck to Germanicus' brother', but the inner circle of the imperial court and aristocratic society generally treated him with contempt. At dinner parties he fell asleep, and other guests threw the pits of olives and dates at him. Sometimes practical jokers put slippers on his hands as he slept in order to watch him rub his face with them when he awoke. He was also prosecuted for forgery and was declared bankrupt. Caligula's treatment of his uncle is sometimes said to have been better than that of Augustus and Tiberius because he let the man hold public office, but the kindness was mixed with a streak of cruelty.[319]

The imperial sisters were another matter. Caligula was devoted to them, tied by bonds of incest and the fear they had felt under Tiberius. On 15 December AD 37, Agrippina gave birth to a son, the future Emperor, Nero. She asked Caligula to give him a name, hoping that he would call the boy Gaius, after himself. Instead the Emperor jestingly proposed the name Claudius, but Agrippina would not name her son after one of the 'jokes of the court'.[320]

It was the eldest sister, Drusilla, who was the Emperor's favourite. During his illness he had named her his heir.[321] Caligula had freed her from her marriage to L. Cassius Longinus and arranged instead for her to marry the much younger Marcus Aemilius Lepidus, a man sometimes referred to as Caligula's lover. Lepidus, as Drusilla's husband, was made heir-designate to the throne.[322] But then tragedy struck, and Drusilla died on 10 June AD 38.[323] Caligula's grief became legendary, and despite the attempts by some modern authors to justify it, grotesquely excessive.[324]

The Senate conferred on Drusilla all the honours that Livia, wife of Augustus and mother of Tiberius, had received. She was given a public funeral, and Lepidus delivered the eulogy. Caligula was too distraught even to attend. The Praetorian Guard was brought out on parade, and the Troy Games were celebrated around her tomb. A period of mourning was declared, and the Emperor forbade all public festivities. Suetonius writes that during the mourning it was a capital offence 'to laugh, bathe, or dine in company with one's parents, wife or children.'[325] Dio reports that one man was executed for treason simply for selling hot water (for mixing with wine). This incident, he says, was 'the key to all that happened at that time'.[326]

The Emperor simply could not tolerate life in Rome, so he left the capital and went south to Naples and Sicily. Unable to attend even to his appearance, during his absence he allowed his hair and beard to grow. When he returned to Rome, by September, he decided that Drusilla should become a goddess. All the formalities were observed. Livius Geminus, member of the Senate, swore that he had seen Drusilla actually ascending into heaven and conversing with the gods. He threw himself into his role and called upon all the gods, including Drusilla herself, to testify to his story. For his brush with divinity he was rewarded with a gift of one million sesterces, and Drusilla was deified on the birthday of Augustus and given the name Panthea, signifying that she possessed the qualities of all the goddesses.[327]

No woman had ever been so honoured, not even Livia, and deification of mortals had actually occurred only twice before in the cases of Caesar and Augustus.[328] There is no doubt that Drusilla was worshipped.[329] She did not receive her own temple because her cult was associated with that of Venus, the special goddess of the Julian clan, and her statue appeared in the temple of Venus, as large as the one of Venus herself. The Senate honoured her by placing her effigy in gold in the Senate House, and it created her own shrine with twenty priests and priestesses. Caligula further stipulated that all women taking oaths should do so in her name, and games were celebrated on her birthday. For the rest of his life the Emperor used no other oath, even before the people and the troops.

There has been some doubt about these facts because no Roman coins commemorate her deification, and there is no further record of her cult or of her shrine in Rome. On the other hand, Roman authors living in a later period testify to these truths, and the absence of physical evidence must be attributed to the fact that Caligula's successor did not promote the cult.[330]

We know that Claudius' cult was ignored in the reign of Nero. In Claudius' case, the Emperor Vespasian restored the cult, but no Emperor after Caligula would have done that for Drusilla.[331] Numerous inscriptions do attest to her shrines in the provinces.[332]

A recent biographer has said, 'What is striking is that [these honours] were granted to a person of such little political significance. But this does not in itself indicate that Caligula was deranged, or under the influence of eastern practices, any more than, say, Queen Victoria in erecting grandiose monuments for the late Prince Albert.'[333] In fact, Roman writers regarded Caligula's actions on the death of his sister as a sign of madness, and there is no reason to believe that they were wrong. What Caligula did was more than just 'excessive', and it certainly was not 'within the bounds of Roman tradition', as least not as far as Roman authors and common sense seem to indicate. Drusilla had not played as important a role in Roman history as Livia or Antonia, yet those two great ladies had not been deified.[334]

Shortly after arranging these matters the Emperor married again for the third time. His bride was Lollia Paulina, the fabulously wealthy wife of a distinguished senator, Publius Memmius Regulus, Governor of Macedonia. One story was that Caligula heard someone say that her grandmother was a remarkably beautiful woman. On hearing the report, the Emperor called Lollia to Rome and married her, forcing her husband to agree to the match. She later became one of the competitors for marriage with Claudius, after the death of Messalina.[335] Her marriage with Caligula was brief; after a few months he divorced her and ordered her never to have sex with another man.[336] In the meantime he had fallen in love with Milonia Caesonia, who was already pregnant with his child.

Remarkably the marriage with Caesonia (in the summer of 39) proved successful. That, at least, is the common view, and she did remain loyal to him to the end, although they lived together only for about one and a half years before their deaths. Caesonia was older than he was and not beautiful, but extravagant and wanton. He loved her passionately and took her with him, out of pride, to review the troops. There was a story that she used aphrodisiacs to keep him attached to her.[337] He allowed his friends to see her nude, and when she bore him a daughter, one month after their marriage, he named the child Drusilla. He knew that she was his child because of her temper – she tried even as an infant to scratch the faces and eyes of her playmates.[338] He carried her as a newborn baby to the temple of Jupiter on the Capitol and placed her on the god's knee and on Minerva's.

The deaths of his father-in-law, Tiberius Gemellus, Macro, and Drusilla, and the rather rapid changes in his own marital status served as a background for the ominous thoughts which must have been swirling through the caverns of his demented mind. Life for him must have been exciting, full of surprises and great suffering. The loss of Drusilla, especially, coming as it did only a few years after the loss of mother and brothers, caused the Emperor enormous grief, and his problems with his wives undoubtedly weighed heavily on him. For one only in his mid-twenties, Caligula had already experienced a lifetime of tragedy and triumph.

For some reason he decided, in 39, to launch a war against the senatorial aristocracy. He had begun his reign by recalling all exiles and destroying all documents revealing any complicity in the previous persecution of members of his family. Although he did not publicly dishonour Tiberius' memory, he made it clear in numerous ways that his own policies would be quite different from his predecessor's and abandoned the use of the law against treason.

As events unfolded it became clear that Caligula had not actually destroyed the incriminating records. Balsdon believed that it 'would have been an act of the wildest folly' for him to have done so.[339] Most Romans seem to have expected him to keep his promises, however, and that should not be surprising. As the Emperor pored over the files, he decided that the blame for his family's suffering rested not with Tiberius but rather with the Senate.

So, early in the year 39 he entered the Senate and gave a frightening speech, praising Tiberius at length and reprimanding the Senate and people for their attitude towards the late Emperor. Caligula said that he, as Emperor, had the right to criticize Tiberius if he pleased, but anyone else who did so was guilty of treason. He then began a review of all the instances under Tiberius when men had been executed, and tried to show that the Senate had been responsible, because senators had made the accusations, senators had been witnesses, and the Senate had voted the condemnation. He even had his freedmen read passages from the documents that were supposed to have been destroyed.[340]

He then added, somewhat inconsistently, 'If Tiberius really did do wrong, you ought not, by Jupiter, to have honoured him while he lived, and then, after repeatedly saying and voting what you did, turn about now. But it was not Tiberius alone that you treated in a fickle manner; Sejanus also you first puffed up with conceit and spoiled, then put him to death.'[341] He then claimed that the spirit of Tiberius had told him, 'In all this you have spoken well and truly. Therefore show no affection for any of them and spare none of them. For they all hate you and they all pray for your death; and they will murder you if they can.'[342]

This remarkable speech caused instant consternation. After finishing it Caligula restored the law of treason, ordered his decree to be inscribed and displayed on a bronze tablet, and the stunned senators simply adjourned. They met the next day, however, and their behaviour revealed the force of imperial tyranny. They praised Caligula as a wonderful Emperor, indicated their gratification that he had not perished as other members of his family had, and voted annual sacrifices to his clemency. They decreed that when the ceremony was celebrated each year, a golden statue of the Emperor should be carried to the Capitol by a procession of youthful aristocrats singing his praises. The historian Dio Cassius adds, 'They also granted him the right to celebrate an ovation, as if he had defeated some enemies.'[343]

By that time Caligula held the Senate and the people in contempt, and he launched a wave of persecutions. Some of the persons who had been recalled from exile were tried again and convicted of the same crime. As Dio Cassius writes, 'In fact, there was nothing but slaughter; for the emperor no longer showed any favours even to the populace, but opposed absolutely everything they wished, and consequently the people on their part resisted all his desires.'[344] Caligula became angry when citizens showed little interest in some of the games, when they did not applaud his favourite performers, and when they honoured some he did not like. It also irritated him to be hailed as 'young Augustus', because he believed it was a criticism of his youth.[345]

He was also sensitive to the fact that his grandfather, Marcus Agrippa, was of non-senatorial origins. He did not want anyone to include Agrippa as an ancestor of the Caesars, and so he claimed that his own mother, Agrippina, was the product of an incestuous affair that Augustus had had with his own daughter, Julia.[346] He also criticized Livia, calling her a 'Ulysses in petticoats', and in a letter to the Senate he accused her of low birth, something that simply was not true.[347]

His persecutions were accompanied by extraordinary cruelty. He liked his victims to be tortured to a slow, agonizing death. He is supposed to have said to the executioners, 'Strike so that he may feel that he is dying', and his favourite statement became, 'Let them hate me as long as they fear me.'[348] At a public banquet, when a slave was discovered stealing some silver, Caligula ordered the executioner to cut off the man's hands, hang them from his neck around his chest, and then lead him among the guests with a placard revealing his crime.[349] He made parents attend the executions of their children, and forced one father to come to dinner immediately afterwards, while the Emperor joked and jested throughout the meal.[350] He ordered the beating of the manager of gladiatorial shows, with chains, over several successive days, and would not kill him until the stench of his putrefied body became too great.[351] One writer was burned alive in the arena because a line he wrote had a double meaning. A Roman equestrian, tossed to the beasts, claimed to be innocent, so Caligula brought him out of the arena, cut out his tongue, and sent him back again.[352] He once demanded that the limbs and bowels of a senatorial victim be stacked in a heap in his presence.[353]

Ancient writers reveal other instances of gross cruelty. Even if some of these stories are untrue or greatly exaggerated, there can be little doubt that Caligula was one of the cruellest rulers Rome ever had, and the competition for that title is great. The Emperor's megalomania was unbounded. He once broke out in a fit of laughter at a banquet, and when the consuls reclining next to him asked what was so humorous, he said that it had just occurred to him that he could remove their heads with a single nod.[354] Suetonius reported that he said to his lovers when he kissed their necks, 'You'll lose this beautiful head whenever I decide.'[355]

A famous incident occurred shortly after the speech he gave to the Senate praising Tiberius. Down by the Bay of Naples Caligula decided to stage an extravaganza. He spurned the Senate's offer of an ovation and ordered his engineers to build a bridge, more than three miles long, spanning the bay from Puteoli to Baiae. For the bridge, merchant ships were anchored together in a double line, and a road modelled on the Appian Way was built across them. So many ships were needed that it was necessary to build some of them, and Dio says that there was a famine in Rome because merchant ships were taken from the grain trade. Resting places and lodging rooms were added to the route of the bridge, complete with running water.[356]

Fortunately the sea remained unusually calm, and Caligula explained that even Neptune was afraid of him. On the first day of the two-day festival he wore the breastplate of Alexander the Great, which had been brought from the conqueror's tomb in Alexandria.[357] He was also decked out with full armour, a purple cloak of cloth of gold, adorned with jewels from India, and a crown of oak leaves. He assembled a force of cavalry and infantry and, after sacrificing to Neptune and to Envy (so that others would not be jealous of him), charged across the bridge. Suetonius reports that he rode back and forth on both days, while Dio Cassius says that the Emperor rode to Baiae on the first day, stayed there for a day, and returned on a chariot on the third day.

On the second day there was a splendid ceremony. Caligula rode out to the centre of the bridge on a chariot drawn by famous racehorses. He was followed by his 'spoils', including a Parthian prince, Darius, who was a hostage in Rome. Numerous high-ranking friends and associates trailed behind, dressed in elaborate attire. At the rear came the Praetorian Guard. The Emperor then addressed the assembled multitude from a platform especially built for the occasion. He praised his own unparalleled achievement in building the bridge and then glorified his troops who had endured so many hardships, including crossing the sea on foot. Afterwards he distributed money to the troops, and then there was a great feast right on the bridge. Some people anchored in their boats nearby, and others were invited from shore to join the party. As the celebrants became drunk, some fell, or were pushed, into the sea, and some even drowned. Fires from the circle of hills around the bridge shone down on the revellers; the Emperor had turned night into day, just as he had turned the sea into land.

Ancient writers treated this episode as an extravagant and wasteful display, but some modern authors have attempted to rationalize it. Balsdon believed that it was done for the benefit of the Parthian hostage, son of the King of Parthia, as a demonstration of Rome's wealth and power. Some Romans thought their Emperor was merely trying to outdo the famous Persian king Xerxes, who had bridged the Hellespont. Others suspected he was trying to intimidate the Celts of Britain and the Germans. Suetonius offered another explanation – that the famous astrologer, Thrasyllus, had once told Tiberius that Caligula had no more chance of becoming Emperor than of riding over the Gulf of Baiae on horseback. The modern rationalization is strained, and the whole affair is more likely to have been simply another whimsical vanity on Caligula's part.[358] Normally a historian can expect to find a rational explanation for everything, since he deals with rational individuals. It is much more difficult to explain the acts of a crazy man.

There followed in Rome a number of famous trials for treason. Calvisius Sabinus, former Governor of Pannonia, was charged with treason along with his wife, and the two committed suicide before the trial. She had been involved in scandal, having committed adultery with Titus Vinius in legionary head-quarters.[359] Titus Rufus was executed for having said that the Senate thought one way and voted another, an obvious reference to senatorial sycophants. The Emperor made money on these charges since the estates of the convicted were confiscated. One aristocrat, Junius Priscus, suffered the supreme penalty, and it was discovered that he was bankrupt. Caligula commented that 'he might just as well have lived.'[360]

The Younger Seneca, famous Stoic philosopher and later tutor to Nero, narrowly escaped death. The Emperor fancied himself an outstanding orator and was jealous of a skilful speech Seneca had given in the Senate. 'Sand without lime' was Caligula's verdict on Seneca's oratory, but the philosopher from Spain survived, because someone told Caligula that he was dying anyway.[361] Another orator, the great Gnaeus Domitius Afer, had observed that Caligula was consul in his twenty-seventh year, and the Emperor, considering that an insulting reference to his youth, personally brought charges against him in the Senate. During the reign of Tiberius, Domitius Afer had incurred the wrath of Caligula's mother, so the Emperor had a grudge against the man. Afer was a famous orator, and Caligula took great pains with his own speech of condemnation. Afer saved himself by claiming to be amazed at the Emperor's skill, praising the oration point by point, claiming to be more afraid of Caligula as an orator than as the Emperor. This appeal to Caligula's vanity worked, and Domitius Afer was acquitted. When a friend asked why Caligula had accused him in the first place, the ruler replied,

'It would not have been right for me to keep such a speech to myself.'[362]

Almost immediately after this episode Caligula removed the two consuls from office because they had not celebrated his birthday properly and because they had celebrated Augustus' victory over Antony at Actium. For some reason Caligula had decided that his descent from Mark Antony was more important than his descent from Augustus.[363] Modern attempts to rationalize this attitude as an effort on Caligula's part to unite the eastern and western halves of the Empire are strained.[364] In any event, the Emperor appointed Domitius Afer to fill one of the vacant consular positions.

In the year from September, 37, to September, 38, Caligula had again experienced much trauma. The death of Drusilla, three marriages, the attack on the Senate, the revival of the law of treason, the deaths of Macro, Tiberius Gemellus, and Junius Silanus, all combined to accelerate the breakdown of a previously tormented mind. Yet the worst was still to come, for the Emperor and for his subjects.

7. Caligula Goes North

Caligula's foreign and defence policies were no less strange than his domestic ones. In the autumn of 39, the Emperor, on a whimsical compulsion, left Italy and crossed the Alps. What transpired on this crazy crusade is one of the strangest stories in Roman history. All ancient authors who refer to it describe Caligula's activities along the Rhine as a fiasco. The historian Tacitus calls them 'a joke' (*ludibrium*).[365] Suetonius believed that Caligula went north in order to replenish the recruits in his German bodyguard, and Dio Cassius said that the Emperor wanted to raise money in Spain and Gaul to replenish a bankrupt treasury.

For whatever reason, Caligula assembled an enormous force of some 200,000 to 250,000 troops and a huge supply of military equipment and food. The Emperor also brought along gladiators, actors and women. He set out from Mevania in Italy at breakneck speed, moving ahead of his bodyguard. When he tired of the effort, he climbed into a litter borne by eight men, and his agents rushed ahead to the towns along the route, forcing the inhabitants to sweep the streets and then sprinkle them to keep down the dust.[366] It was probably at this time that Caligula replaced two of the three legions that had been lost at the Battle of the Teutoburg Forest.[367] He reached Mainz on the Rhine after a journey of about forty days, a remarkably fast trip considering the distance, nearly one thousand Roman miles.[368] After the arrival he was furious with some of his generals who had not yet reached headquarters. Not much later he dismissed them along with some high-ranking centurions who were nearing retirement. Then he reduced the retirement benefits of the other troops by half.[369] One ancient report indicates that Caligula took vengeance on the troops who had threatened him and his mother in the mutiny of AD 14; there were probably still a few of them left in the service as late as AD 40.[370]

No Emperor had visited the provinces in more than fifty years, but both Augustus and Tiberius had considerable experience with provincial affairs long before they became Emperor. It was not necessary for them to demonstrate their connection with the troops, since they had spent many years in legionary head-quarters. Caligula may have been a child of the camps, and his father had won the support of the army, but the Emperor lacked personal military service. There is no evidence, however, that his visit to the Rhine was a matter of policy, a trip designed to strengthen the military underpinning of the Julio-Claudian dynasty. Indeed, Caligula's adventure on the Rhine cannot have done anything but undermine the legions' adherence to the regime.

The Emperor had taken his sisters, Agrippina and Livilla, with him as well as Aemilius Lepidus, still his heir-designate. Shortly after arriving at Mainz, however, he executed Lepidus on grounds of conspiring with the commander of the legions of Upper Germany, Lentulus Gaetulicus. Gaetulicus had an interesting history. He received his appointment as Governor of Upper Germany in 30, while Sejanus was influential in Tiberius' government, and we can assume that he was one of Sejanus' friends. In the reign of terror against the political allies of the Praetorian Prefect, after his fall from power, Gaetulicus was accused. He was the only person closely associated with Sejanus who escaped condemnation, and Tacitus said that he did so by writing to Tiberius and pointing out that even the Emperor had been duped by the Prefect. The ambitious Gaetulicus proposed to Tiberius that they agree that the Governor would keep his province and the Emperor would keep his empire.[371]

Whatever the truth of that rumour, Gaetulicus was still Governor of Upper Germany when Caligula arrived in the autumn of 39. He was popular with his troops and with the legions of Lower Germany which were commanded by his father-in-law, L. Apronius. Some scholars believe that Gaetulicus was a lax disciplinarian, but the passage cited in Tacitus for confirmation does not actually say that.[372] What it does say is that the Governor was '*modicus severitate*' – meaning roughly 'moderate in his severity (or harshness)'. Tacitus did not accuse Gaetulicus of lax discipline in his command; indeed, the historian's comments are generally favourable to the Governor and seem to imply that his legionary support was strong enough to threaten Tiberius.[373] He did not suggest that Gaetulicus had been an incompetent governor.

It does appear that Aemilius Lepidus and Gaetulicus conspired to overthrow Caligula. His sisters were also involved in the plot, and Agrippina had apparently become the lover of Lepidus.[374] The two ringleaders were executed, while the sisters were banished to islands (although they were warned that the Emperor had swords as well as islands). Agrippina was first forced to carry the urn containing Lepidus' ashes in her arms back to Rome. Lepidus' throat had been cut by a tribune, and the Senate decreed that his remains should not be given proper burial.[375] At the trial the Emperor had produced letters that clearly implicated all parties to the conspiracy.[376] There is no direct evidence to support the view, argued forcefully by Balsdon, that Caligula learned of this conspiracy before leaving Italy and that the discovery was the cause of his removal of the two consuls and their replacement by people he could trust.[377] Nor is there any reason to believe that the Emperor's knowledge of the conspiracy explains his abrupt departure and rapid journey. No matter how fast the imperial party travelled, it could not even come close to the speed of the post. Caligula could not have taken Gaetulicus by surprise, and no ancient author supports the modern rationalization of Caligula's actions.[378] There was, however, a genuine conspiracy, and it is possible that the Emperor was thrown off balance by the involvement of the three people most dear to him, after his wife Caesonia.

Why Agrippina, Livilla, Lepidus and Gaetulicus conspired to

overthrow Caligula is nowhere revealed in the ancient sources. There has been much modern speculation, and every conceivable reason except the most obvious one has had its adherents. What probably happened is that the people closest to the Emperor – Agrippina, Livilla, and Lepidus – had come to the conclusion that Caligula simply could no longer be tolerated, and was showing increasing signs of instability. We know from subsequent events under Claudius and Nero that Agrippina was ambitious, and her brother's behaviour offered some scope for her own aspirations. On the other hand, the three members of the family had real affection for the troubled Emperor. Lepidus and Caligula had been lovers. When Agrippina and Livilla returned from exile after Claudius came to power, the first thing they did was to tend to their brother's remains.[379]

Despite their personal attachment to Caligula, members of his family realized that the Emperor had to be overthrown. The marriage with Caesonia muddied the dynastic waters to a certain extent, and Lepidus' position as heir-designate was somewhat clouded by the possibility that the Emperor's wife might bear a son.[380] Gaetulicus, as the most powerful military commander along the Rhine, made an obvious ally, and he had revealed his independence under Tiberius. Claudius was not taken seriously by anyone and did not figure into the scheming. Caligula's wild antics and irrational behaviour threatened the regime, and the high-ranking members of the family had to do something or risk losing everything. Unfortunately we do not know how Caligula discovered the conspiracy soon enough to counteract it.

The Emperor's subsequent actions along the Rhine were a source of wonder and merriment to ancient authors, who universally saw them as crazy. Considering the vast force Caligula had assembled, it is likely that he had originally planned a very extensive campaign, possibly pursuing his father's dream of conquering Germany to the Elbe. Perhaps the conspiracy unsettled him so much that he could not carry out his plans. Suetonius reports that Caligula found no one to fight, so he sneaked a few of his German bodyguards across the Rhine and had them hidden. After the Emperor finished lunch at headquarters, news was brought to him in a show of surprise and confusion that the enemy was nearby. Caligula then rushed out with his friends and mounted members of the Praetorian Guard, cut branches from trees nearby and decorated the trunks like trophies. Then he returned to camp after nightfall, by torchlight. The Emperor chastized those who had not followed him, calling them cowards, and gave to the members of his party crowns that were adorned with figures of the sun, moon, and stars.

On another occasion, Suetonius reports, hostages were taken from a school and secretly positioned some distance ahead of the Emperor. Then Caligula suddenly left a dinner, rushed out with cavalry, bound the hostages, and brought them back in chains. He returned to find that the troops had been assembled, and he made them take their seats in armour, quoting a line from Virgil that they should 'bear up and save themselves for other things.'[381] He then criticized the Senate and people for enjoying themselves at the games and the theatres while Caesar was exposed to the dangers of battle.[382] Dio Cassius says that Caligula won no battles, killed no enemies, and merely captured a few 'by a ruse'. Despite this, he was hailed *imperator* by the troops seven times.[383]

After this bizarre autumn on the Rhine Caligula withdrew to the city of Lyon in central Gaul to spend the winter. In Rome the Arval Brethren had met on 27 October, 39, to offer thanks for the discovery of the conspiracy against the Emperor. Although many senators may have privately wished that the conspiracy had been successful, publicly they voted the Emperor an ovation and sent a committee of their body to offer Caligula personal congratulations. Caesar's uncle Claudius was selected to head the delegation. The Emperor had ordered that no member of his family should be honoured after his sisters and Lepidus had conspired against him, and he was furious with the Senate for sending Claudius.[384] Caligula ranted that the Senate had sent his uncle as though he were in need of a guardian, and there is a story that he threw Claudius into the river, fully clothed.[385]

The Senate sent a new and larger delegation, and this time Caligula received it warmly. In the meantime the Emperor had ordered that all his sisters' personal possessions, jewels and furniture, be sent to him in Lyon. He put them up for auction and made a fortune. At the sale Caesar held items up and said such things as, 'This belonged to my father', or 'This belonged to my mother', or 'Augustus got this from Antony.' The richest men of Gaul and others in the Emperor's retinue purchased many valuable imperial heirlooms. The business was so profitable that Caligula ordered many objects to be brought from the parts of the palace that Augustus and Tiberius had previously occupied. According to Suetonius, the Emperor requisitioned transport animals from the public carriages and the bakeries to bring the valuables to Lyon, and as a result it was difficult to get bread in Rome, and some people could not get to court for their cases.[386]

As an auctioneer Caligula was superb. He cajoled the bidders, accusing them of avarice, of wanting to be richer than he was. At the same time he lamented that commoners were buying the property of princes. Naturally everyone bought at prices far higher than the objects were actually worth. One rich provincial had bribed Caligula's staff to be invited to an imperial dinner party, paying the extravagant amount of two hundred thousand sesterces. When Caligula found out about this, he was pleased that anyone was willing to spend so much to dine with him. The next morning at the auction, he sent a courier to give the man an insignificant item for the price of two hundred thousand sesterces and invite him to dinner at Caesar's personal request.[387]

By this time he was obviously bankrupt. He had frittered away the vast surplus left by Tiberius and was trying to raise revenues in any way he could. Dio Cassius reports that while he was gambling at Lyon, he ran out of money, asked his assistants to bring the census lists of Gaul (which also contained property assessments), and ordered the wealthiest men to be put to death. When he returned to the game, he told the other players, 'While you play here for a few *denarii*, I have just made one hundred and fifty million.'[388]

In Rome members of the Senate brought prosecutions against the Emperor's enemies, friends of his sisters. Naturally there were many of them, because it had been fashionable to associate with the imperial family. Sofonius Tigellinus, who would become famous under Nero, was one of the exiles, accused of adultery with Agrippina. Even some office-holders, who should have been immune from prosecution during their year in power, were forced to resign and stand trial. The Senate and people were alarmed at this witch-hunt. For a while in January of 40 no one could be found to convene the Senate. Caesar was sole consul, and during his absence, no governmental official was willing to act in his place. On 1 January the Senate did, however, proceed in a body to the Capitol, paid homage to Caligula, retired to the Senate House, and spent the day praising the Emperor, even though they had not been officially convened. As Dio Cassius said, 'For since they had no love for him nor any wish that he should survive, they went to greater lengths in simulating these feelings, as if hoping in this way to disguise their real feelings.'[389]

On 3 January all the Praetors in a joint announcement convened the Senate, so that no single one of them would be in jeopardy, and senators spent the day in prayer, again conducting no business. It was not until 12 January that news reached Rome that Caesar had resigned as consul, and then new consuls were sworn in, and the Senate was convened. One measure the senators approved was a motion requiring the birthdays of Drusilla and Tiberius to be celebrated in the same manner as that of Augustus. Even this was done at the Emperor's request.[390]

Meanwhile in Lyon, except among the wealthy, who were subject to Caesar's exactions, there was great excitement. The personal presence of the Emperor was a major event for a provincial city, and Caligula did his best not to disappoint. There were various games, including one unusual one, a contest in Greek and Latin oratory, perhaps reflecting the Emperor's personal interest in that art. In any event, even this contest had an odd twist. The losers were forced to present the prizes to the winners and to compose poems of praise for them. The defeated contestants had to erase their contributions, some with a sponge and the worst with their tongues. As an alternative they were permitted to choose a beating with rods or to be thrown into the river.[391] In the second century the poet Juvenal commemorated this competition in one of his satires:

> Let each take the price of his blood
> and turn pale in consequence
> As a man who steps barefoot on a snake
> or waits in suspense
> To give an oration at the harrowing
> Lyons contest.[392]

It is unlikely that the citizens of Lyon were terribly disappointed when Caligula left the city to assemble his army on the coast of Gaul for an invasion of Britain. The return of the Emperor to the camps was hardly a source of comfort to the troops either. The soldiers of Upper Germany certainly did not like their new commander, Galba, the future Emperor, whose reputation for strict discipline proved justified.[393] Gaetulicus had been popular, but Galba made it clear on the first day after he arrived in the region that there was a new regime. When the troops applauded at a festival, he issued orders for them to keep their hands under their cloaks. There would be no nonsense tolerated. The combination of a strict disciplinarian and a crazy emperor must have been unsettling to the legions.

Why Caligula decided to invade Britain no one knows. The loss of Tacitus' account of the reign is particularly critical at this point, since the historian had a special interest in Britain because his father-in-law, Agricola, had campaigned there. Julius Caesar had crossed the Channel twice in the summers of 55 and 54 BC, and the romantic incursions had attracted considerable attention in Rome, but neither Augustus nor Tiberius showed any inclination to attempt a conquest of the island. There was no good strategic or economic reason to add Britain to the Roman Empire, and when it was finally conquered, the province required a permanent garrison of three legions, about one tenth of the disposable forces available to the Emperor.[394]

Caligula had already been given the name Britannicus by the Senate before he left Lyon.[395] Earlier, after his arrival on the Rhine in the autumn of 39, the British prince Amminus (Adminius) had deserted to the Romans. At that time Caligula sent a spectacular letter, which, on his precise instructions, was to be delivered personally to the consuls in the temple of Mars before a full meeting of the Senate. The Emperor treated the defection of Amminus as the equivalent of the conquest of the island, and it was probably at that time that he received the title Britannicus.[396]

The account of Caligula's abortive invasion of Britain is one of the most curious in Roman history.[397] Unfortunately, in addition to the loss of Tacitus' version, the manuscript of Dio Cassius is also defective at this point in his narrative, and we depend on a later abridgement by Xiphilinus for his account. However, since it is approximately the same as the one surviving by Suetonius, and since we know from passing comments in other sections of Tacitus that he considered the 'invasion' a miserable failure, we probably are in possession of the ancient view of Caligula's so-called campaign.

What Suetonius says is that the Emperor assembled his forces on the Channel, facing Britain.[398] After arranging his catapults and other engines of war, he embarked on a trireme but turned back after moving only a short distance. Both Dio and Suetonius indicate that the troops were confused, uncertain of what the Emperor planned to do. Upon returning to the shore, Caligula took position on a high tower or lighthouse especially built for the occasion and commanded the trumpeters to sound the charge. Caesar then suddenly urged them to pick up shells along the coast, using their helmets and the folds of their clothing to gather them. He announced that they were 'spoils from the sea' (*spolia Oceani*) and dedicated the lighthouse in commemoration of his victory, rivalling the famous lighthouse of Pharos in Alexandria, one of the Seven Wonders of the Ancient World.[399]

The Emperor of Rome, who had somewhat prematurely been granted the name Britannicus, decided that he would settle for a triumph and merely display the shells for the delight of the people. He added a few captives and deserters from the Gauls, selected the tallest among them as 'worthy of a triumph', added a few chiefs, and then made them grow their hair long and dye it red. The 'prisoners' were then forced to learn a little of a Germanic language, and they assumed barbarian names. The squadron of triremes that he had led into the sea was carried overland to Rome.[400] Before leaving for the capital, Caligula decided to punish the legions that had mutinied under his father, Germanicus, and he ordered them to be decimated after he was persuaded that he could not butcher them all. But when he saw that they were likely to resist by force of arms, he hastily abandoned the idea and returned to Rome.[401]

The story of Caligula's 'campaigns' in the North in the winter of 39–40 is so farcical and outrageous that modern historians tend to reject it, and they look instead for a rational explanation of parts of it. Balsdon speculated that the saga of the seashells grew out of a misunderstanding of a military technical term. The Latin word for shells is *musculi*, but the same word may be used for the sappers' huts that were needed in sieges. Balsdon wrote, '. . . the whole story of the command to pick up shells may have grown out of a civilian's misunderstanding of what, at any rate in Caesar's time, appears to have been a rare technical word.'[402]

On the face of it, however, that seems highly unlikely.[403] Surely there were Romans living in the time between Suetonius and Dio Cassius who would have detected that error and drawn attention to it. But the main argument against modern attempts to rationalize the ancient version of Caligula's activities in the North is that almost every aspect of the story has to be explained or dismissed. It is possible to believe that the ancient authors got some of their facts wrong; we know that they did. But it is one thing to try to make sense out of the ancient tradition about a normally intelligent ruler – a regular and necessary technique of modern historians – and quite another to find a semblance of order in the acts of a crazy man. It is almost always possible to do that, and the result can be misleading.

Caligula actually planned to invade Britain, but he aborted the project for various reasons. His failure in Germany, the serious conspiracy of Lepidus and Gaetulicus, and fear of growing senatorial hostility in Rome all undoubtedly played a part. But there is also simply an element of insanity in his behaviour in the North. The Emperor of Rome was losing his grip, and he may well have sensed the fact, causing him to act more erratically than he might otherwise have done.

Caligula's life, which had been played out from childhood on a highly dramatic stage, continued in the period from autumn 39 to spring 40 to be one of great tension. In those months he executed his heir-designate and lover, Lepidus. He banished his two surviving sisters for their complicity in a plot to topple him, a conspiracy that had the support of one of his strongest military commanders, Gaetulicus. His own military campaigns ended in comedy, and his sojourn at Lyon left an unfortunate impression in the provinces. As his reign approached its final crescendo of folly, Romans waited in fear to see what would happen.

8. The Big Humbug

Caligula reached the environs of Rome in May, 40. He participated in a ceremony of the Arval Brethren on 29 May and headed south to Campania. He did not actually enter the city of Rome until 31 August when he celebrated his ovation, rather than a formal triumph. It is not certain why he remained out of Rome for so long, but Dio Cassius says that the weather that summer was so hot that awnings were stretched across the Forum, and this may have been a factor.[404] It is also possible that he was afraid that his enemies in the Senate would assassinate him.

The Emperor had indicated as he left the North that he no longer respected the Senate. Indeed, he went further and made open threats; Seneca says that he considered killing all senators.[405] He complained that he had been cheated out of his triumph, although he had earlier forbidden the Senate to honour him. When he was met by a delegation of the Senate, he said that he would return as quickly as possible and that he was bringing his sword with him. He would return only to those who wanted him, Caesar added, saying that he would no longer be either a citizen or a prince to the Senate.[406]

While in Campania he considered the possibility of transferring the imperial capital from Rome to his birthplace, Antium, or to Alexandria. He kept two notebooks with the names of people who were destined for death. One list was called 'Sword' and the other 'Dagger', depending on how he planned to kill them. He accumulated so many poisons that when they were thrown into the sea on the orders of his successor, Claudius, they caused dead fish to be tossed up onto the shore.[407] Yet his policies, such as they were, were inconsistent. He had restored the elections to the people, but he gave them back to the Senate, because the people had not exercised their rights.[408] When he did enter Rome, he tossed money to the crowds from a roof, causing a stampede that left heavy casualties – 32 men, 247 women, and one eunuch, according to a late imperial source. He was accused of mixing small pieces of iron with the coins to stir up the throng.[409]

Suetonius says that Caligula 'added to the enormity of his crimes by the brutality of his language'.[410] The Emperor personally claimed to be utterly shameless and proud of the fact. Once an ex-Praetor went on leave to a small town because of illness. When he asked Caligula for an extension of the leave, the Emperor sent an agent to kill him, saying that if he had not been helped by his long medical treatment, he needed to be bled. Caligula once deplored the fact that there had been no great tragedies in his reign, such as the massacre of the legions under Varus. He yearned for famine, epidemic, fires or earthquakes, so that his reign might not be forgotten because of its prosperity.

At this time (the autumn of 40) there were many conspiracies, and the plotters were executed with a vengeance. Combining stories from Dio Cassius and Seneca, it would appear that four senators, Betilienus Bassus, Sextus Papinius and two Anicii Ceriales (father and son), conspired against the Emperor with other associates.[411] They were all subjected to torture, and the younger Anicius Cerialis broke down and received a pardon by becoming an informer on the others, including his own father. The other three were executed, and the father of Betilienus Bassus, Betilienus Capito, was ordered by Caligula to attend the execution. When the father asked whether he could close his eyes, the Emperor ordered him to be executed also. Capito then implicated the Prefects of the Guard, one of the imperial freedmen, Callistus, and Caesar's wife, Caesonia, but Caligula refused to believe that Caesonia would turn against him, and he ignored the accusation.

In capital cases he liked to conduct the examination by torture while he was eating or having a party.[412] He once stood beside the statue of Jupiter and asked the famous actor, Apelles, which of the two was greater, Jupiter or Caesar. Apelles, at a loss for words, a rare thing for an actor, hesitated. The Emperor had him whipped. When Apelles asked for mercy, Caligula complimented him on his refinement, even while groaning.[413]

The Emperor sought public attention and was unafraid of notoriety. His dress was sometimes shocking; he wore cloaks decorated with valuable gems, sometimes wore slippers, and occasionally put on the boots of his German bodyguard. He seems to have been a transvestite, dressing now and then as a goddess and at other times merely as a mortal woman.[414] At the theatre the Emperor tried to join in the plays, and he considered becoming an actor himself.[415] His whole life-style was exotic and extravagant. Once he summoned three of the leading members of the Senate to the palace at night. They were afraid, and did not know what to expect, but all Caligula did was perform a dance for them, accompanied by musicians, dressed in a cloak and tunic that reached to his heels. He bathed in hot and cold baths of perfumed oils, and he once placed before his guests golden loaves of bread and meat, saying that a man ought either to be frugal or Caesar.[416]

One of his most extravagant acts was to have built some galleys decorated with jewels and coloured sails, containing large baths, colonnades, and banquet rooms. Planted on the vessels were many varieties of vines and fruit trees. The Emperor gave great parties on these ships, sometimes sailing along the coast by Naples while the guests sang songs.[417] Some Roman ships have been recovered from Lake Nemi in the vicinity of Rome which were built in the reign of Caligula, and they confirm Suetonius' account. Equipped with running water, they were heavily decorated, and the floors had mosaics. There were painted scenes, mosaics, and marble on the walls, and many bronze objects throughout.[418]

Meanwhile, the persecutions continued. Another victim of Caligula's tyranny was Julius Graecinus, father of the famous Roman general, Agricola. According to Seneca, his crime was that he was such a good man that his presence embarrassed the Emperor.[419] Graecinus, a philosopher and man of letters, had earlier offended the Emperor by refusing to prosecute Marcus Silanus.[420]

A Roman equestrian by the name of Pastor had a son who offended the Emperor because he was too splendidly dressed and wore his hair in an elaborate style. Caligula imprisoned him, and when the father begged for his son's life, Caligula ordered him to be killed immediately and then invited the father to dinner. Pastor came, drank wine with the Emperor, and had to return again on the day of his son's burial. Once more the father acted as if nothing had happened, but Seneca, who was a contemporary of the period and was writing at a time when there were many alive who might have challenged him, explained that the father's composure was due to the fact that he had another son, and he did not want to imperil that son's future.[421]

One of the Emperor's assistants, a man by the name of Protogenes, who carried Caligula's 'Sword' and 'Dagger' hit-lists, entered the Senate, and as he was greeted by the senators, he turned to Scribonius Proculus and said, 'Do you dare to greet me when you hate the Emperor as much as you do?' His fellow senators tore the hapless Proculus limb from limb.[422] After that outburst, Caesar declared that he was pleased with the Senate, and there was a brief reconciliation. The Senate voted that the Emperor should sit on a raised seat, so that no one could approach him, and that he should be free to bring his military guard into the Senate House.[423] Caligula may have increased the size of the Praetorian Guard from nine to twelve cohorts at this time.[424]

The harmonious interlude did not last long, because it was at about this time that Caligula announced that he was a god. He had become convinced of his own divinity, according to Dio, because '. . . when some called him a demigod and others a god, he fairly lost his head.'[425] It is true that a Roman emperor was routinely subjected to an incredible amount of flattery. All emperors were considered gods in the Hellenistic East, where the inhabitants of the Empire had always worshipped their rulers. Although Augustus and Tiberius had suppressed any attempt to worship them in Rome and Italy, the imperial cult had been encouraged in the provinces. Caligula, even as a mortal, had lived in the company of gods. His great-grandfather, Augustus, had been deified as well as his great-great-grandfather, Julius Caesar; and his sister, Drusilla, had become a goddess. Given a little mental instability, it is not difficult to see why Caligula believed in his own divinity.

Nevertheless, the stories told by ancient authors stagger the imagination. After first imitating some of the minor deities, Caligula claimed that he conversed with and made love to the Moon, and that Victory had actually crowned him.[426] He pretended at one time or another to be Jupiter, Neptune, Hercules, Bacchus, and Apollo. Sometimes he carried a club and wore a lion's skin, at other times he held a trident or a thunderbolt. He even used wigs to create the right divine appearance. Nor did he limit himself to the male deities; he also dressed to impersonate Juno, Diana, and Venus.[427]

In connection with this Dio Cassius tells a wonderful story: 'Once a Gaul, seeing him uttering oracles from a lofty platform in the guise of Jupiter, was moved to laughter, whereupon Gaius summoned him and inquired, "What do I seem to you to be?" And the other answered (I give his exact words): "A big humbug". Yet the man met with no harm, for he was only a shoemaker.'[428]

It was at this time that the Emperor introduced prostration to the court. One of the most important provincial governors of the day, Lucius Vitellius, a man who had faced the king of Parthia without fear, was recalled to Rome and threatened with execution. Vitellius went to Caligula, fell at the Emperor's feet, treated him as a god, and in so doing won a reprieve. This incident started the custom of prostration in the Emperor's presence. Caligula was so pleased with Vitellius that they became close friends. Once, when Caesar was talking to the Moon, he asked Vitellius whether he could see the goddess.

Vitellius averted his eyes, looked to the ground, and said, 'Only you gods, Master, can see one another.'[429]

Seneca reported another notorious instance of prostration. Pomponius Pennus, an ex-consul, came to trial for treason. His mistress, an actress by the name of Quintilia, was tortured severely, but she refused to betray him and was rewarded by Caligula for her bravery with a gift of money. Pomponius was spared but under humiliating conditions:

Caligula gave Pomponius the gift of life, if you can call it a gift, when all he did was not take it away. Then, after Pomponius was pardoned and began to thank the Emperor, Caligula put out his left foot to be kissed. . . . This man, born merely to change the customs of a free people into Persian slavery, considered it insufficient that the senator, an old man who had held the highest offices, threw himself down in the presence of his Emperor in the same way that the vanquished do before their conquerors. He found a way of pushing Liberty down below the knees. Doesn't this trample on the state – and with the left foot, too (though that may not seem important to everyone)! He would not have been crazy and ugly enough, this man who heard a capital case against a former consul, if he had not stuck his slippered foot into the face of a senator![430]

Senatorial sycophants had little alternative but to humour their insane Emperor, but the wealth of information about his pretended relations with the gods shows how shocked his contemporaries were. Caligula's sacrilegious behaviour may sometimes have been amusing, but it often caused consternation. On one occasion, when the Emperor was at the Circus watching pantomimists, thunder interrupted the performance. Caligula became angry and challenged Jupiter to a duel. 'What madness! (*Quanta dementia fuit*!)' said Seneca, 'I think this was instrumental in inciting conspirators against him.'[431]

Actually Caligula claimed a special affinity with Jupiter Capitolinus. He built new quarters on the Capitoline in order to live next to his 'brother' Jupiter. Even more outrageously, he constructed a temple for himself on the Palatine and ordered that the famous statue of Zeus at Olympia, made by the great Greek sculptor, Pheidias, be brought to Rome. This statue was one of the Seven Wonders of the Ancient World, and Caligula planned to remove the head and replace it with a portrayal of his own! Fortunately, Regulus, the Governor of Achaea, told the Emperor that the statue would be ruined if disassembled for transport to Rome.[432]

Still, the temple to Caligula on the Palatine became a major project. The Emperor cut in two the temple of Castor and Pollux in the Forum and ran a road through it to the palace on the Palatine, where he was building his own, claiming that he had the twin gods as his gate-keepers. He claimed to be Jupiter Latiaris, and he appointed as priests his wife Caesonia, his uncle, Claudius, and other aristocrats willing to pay ten million sesterces for the honour. He even made himself and his favourite horse, Incitatus, priests of his own cult.[433] In *The Lives of the Twelve Caesars* Suetonius describes the temple as follows:

> He also set up a special temple to his own godhead, with priests and with victims of the choicest kind. In this temple was a life-sized statue of the Emperor in gold, which was dressed each day in clothing such as he wore himself. The richest citizens used all their influence to secure the priesthoods of his cult and bid high for the honour. The victims were flamingos, peacocks, woodcock, guinea-hens and pheasants, offered day by day each after its own kind.[434]

Another temple to the Emperor in Rome was approved by the Senate to be built with public money, but we do not know its location. In the provinces Caligula advanced his cult by annexing the temple the Milesians were building for Apollo in their territory, about ten miles south of Miletus.[435] Strabo called the temple the largest in the world, and there is an ancient inscription from the site attesting to the existence of a cult of Caligula.[436] Naturally, most of the cults and buildings connected with them in the Empire were not maintained after the Emperor's death, so there is little physical evidence, and we must rely on ancient authors for our knowledge of Caligula's policies.

Some modern authors have refused to believe the tradition about Caligula's self-deification. The major sources, Philo the Jew, Seneca, Josephus, Suetonius, and Dio Cassius were clearly hostile to the Emperor. Balsdon accused them of writing '. . . as if Gaius wilfully imposed his claims to divinity upon a startled world.'[437] Barrett claims that if there was an official cult of Caligula at Rome, which, he writes, 'can certainly not be ruled out', it nevertheless 'would reflect a breach of tradition and protocol rather than a manifestation of madness'.[438] Although it is true that emperor worship did not begin with Caligula, no previous Roman ruler had ever claimed divinity in Rome and Italy. Julius Caesar, Augustus, and Caligula's sister Drusilla had been deified by the Senate only after their deaths. Tiberius had forbidden provincials in Spain to build a temple to himself and his mother.[439]

In the Hellenistic East the situation was different. There inhabitants of the Empire were accustomed to worship their rulers, and it would have been difficult to suppress the tendency. Yet it is not the emperor worship of the East that is at issue here. Caligula went much further than his predecessors in Rome itself. Balsdon blamed the Senate for Caligula's boldness:

> Not only was it impossible to satisfy all critics; it was scarcely possible to avoid the pitfalls which senatorial cunning placed in the Emperor's path. It was a favourite trick of the personal enemies of the Princeps to press upon him honours so distasteful to the majority of reasonably minded men that, if he accepted them, he inevitably swelled the ranks of his adversaries.[440]

Of course that is true, but all emperors learned early to be careful about honours. One thing about the reign of Caligula that is so noticeable is that he eliminated the men of wisdom and experience who might have served as his councillors. Unlike Nero, Caligula had no Seneca to guide him; he killed those around him who might have performed that role – most notably his father-in-law Silanus and his Praetorian Prefect Macro. Within a year of his assumption of power the young Caesar made it clear that he would brook no constraints on his imperial freedom.

Caligula's megalomania essentially knew no bounds. He readily accepted the designation *Optimus Maximus Caesar* – the Best and Greatest Caesar – when he had no claim to the title whatsoever.[441] His father Germanicus had known better. On the trip to Egypt that so offended Tiberius, Germanicus had instructed the Egyptians to keep their honours within reasonable bounds: 'Your goodwill, which you always show whenever you see me, I welcome, but your invidious and god-like appellations I utterly reject. . . . If you do not do as I say, you will force me to appear before you but seldom.'[442]

One reason why many modern scholars are inclined to dismiss the stories of Caligula's claim to divinity is that ancient paganism has not always been taken seriously as a religion. Again Balsdon's words provide the best example:

The contemporary Roman notion of the Olympian godhead was neither ethical, like Philo's, nor mystical, but anthropomorphic, a photographic image of the costume and attributes normally attached to the god's statue. That any thinking man believed in the physical or metaphysical reality of these gods is unlikely. How far Augustus himself believed in the existence of these gods whose reality had been exploded four hundred years earlier by Greek philosophy will never be known. Augustus was too good a censor of his own feelings to reveal the truth.[443]

In recent years, however, students have come to realize that the Romans took their religion very seriously indeed and that it had a strong moral and ethical component, as well as a mystical one.[444] Sacrilege and blasphemy were as shocking to most Romans as they are to Christians and Jews. Caligula's behaviour cannot be excused on the grounds that ancient paganism was merely a fanciful game that nobody took seriously as a religion. Seneca's comment that Caligula's blasphemy of Jupiter was a prime cause of the conspiracy against him deserves a better hearing.

Although one biographer has said that Caligula's claim to divinity was 'hardly a sign of madness',[445] it is difficult to escape the conclusion that the Emperor was growing more and more insane as his reign progressed. The introduction of prostration and emperor worship in Rome was not actually the result of calculated policy, and there is little evidence that Caligula pursued either systematically. Caligula was no Stalin or Hitler; he lacked their consistent ruthlessness and commitment to policy. He was crazy, and his actions were much more whimsical and arbitrary than those of twentieth-century dictators. There was no way of knowing what he might do.

9. Caligula and the Jews

Caligula's antics came very near to provoking rebellion among the Jews. Although the Emperor's attitude towards the gods clearly shocked Greek and Roman pagans, especially Italians, some of his ideas were anathema to the Jews. The young Caesar's departure from the traditional accommodation Rome had made with the Jews led to a crisis that was aborted only by the Emperor's death.[446]

Rome's relationship with the Jews had been based on a number of compromises worked out by Augustus and Tiberius with Jewish leaders. The compromises were both political and religious. Although Tacitus' account of the reign of Caligula is lost, in that historian's famous summary of Jewish history in another work, he writes, 'Under Tiberius all was quiet. But when the Jews were ordered by Caligula to set up his statue in the temple, they preferred the alternative of war. The death of the Emperor put an end to the disturbance.'[447]

Tacitus' cryptic reference to the reign of Caligula left much unsaid. The desecration of the Temple was only one of several problems provoked by Caligula's arrogance. He also tried to inject himself in an unacceptable way into the synagogues, and he did not deal effectively with a controversy between Greeks and Jews in Alexandria. One important fact to remember is that there were as many Jews living in the other provinces of the Empire as there were in Judaea. Caligula has the distinction of being one of the few emperors to have had problems with both groups of Jews at the same time.

Under Augustus the Jews of Palestine were subjected to the rule of Herod the Great, a cruel but intelligent king, who somehow managed to stay in the Emperor's favour and to rule over his people, buffering them in their relations with Rome. Anti-Semitism among the Romans was relatively strong. Normally Romans were tolerant of the religions of their subjects, but Judaism, because of its strongly monotheistic nature, presented a challenge to their toleration. The Jews condemned idolatry and objected even to Roman coins, since they bore the image of the Emperor or members of his family.

The Roman government, however, did recognize the legitimacy of the Jewish religion. Like paganism, Judaism was 'ancestral', that is, it went back into early unrecorded times. Romans understood that, and they later differentiated between Judaism, which was ancestral, and Christianity, which was not. It was a crime to be a Christian in the Roman Empire, but it was not a crime to be a Jew. It was, however, despite that fact, very difficult to practise Judaism because of anti-Semitism on the part of the Gentile population in general and, occasionally, on the part of officials in the Roman government.

When Herod the Great died in 4 BC, Augustus named Herod's son, Archelaus, Ethnarch of Judaea (not King, as his father had been). Ten years later, the Emperor called Archelaus to Rome and banished him to Vienne in Gaul. Judaea became an imperial province ruled by an equestrian Prefect from Caesarea Sebaste rather than Jerusalem. Although the Prefect had no legions under his command, he did have some auxiliary units, and he could always ask the Governor of Syria for additional military support. Realizing that the situation in Judaea was tense, Roman emperors tried to keep a low military profile.

The Jews had been allowed a special coinage without the image of the Emperor. They also objected to the standards of the army, because they bore representations of the ruler, so the standards were modified. The Roman government allowed the Jewish Sanhedrin to exercise its traditional powers, requiring only that capital punishment be approved by the Prefect, who also annually appointed the High Priest. For the most part, this system worked well, but not all Prefects were equally good.

Pontius Pilate held the position in the last ten years of the reign of Tiberius, and he probably was one of Sejanus' supporters.[448] Sejanus was notably anti-Semitic, and Pontius Pilate was not a popular Prefect.[449] Lucius Vitellius, Governor of Syria, removed Pilate from his position late in the reign of Tiberius, and Caligula appointed a new Prefect, Marullus, early in his reign.[450]

The death of Herod the Great, however, had resulted in other administrative changes in the area. Part of Herod's territory was handed over to his son, Philip, and another part, including Galilee, to another son, Herod Antipas. They ruled as Tetrarchs, a somewhat less prestigious title than that of their eldest brother, the Ethnarch Archelaus. Philip was popular, but when he died in 34, his lands were annexed into the province of Syria. Herod Antipas was much less popular. He was married to Herodias, mother of Salome, and it was he who executed John the Baptist. Christ referred to Antipas as 'that fox'.[451] When Vitellius negotiated a major alliance between Rome and Parthia late in 37, after Caligula's accession, Herod Antipas offended the Roman Governor by getting news of the diplomatic coup to the Emperor before Vitellius' own version reached Rome.

These developments set the stage for the appearance of Herod Agrippa as a major player in the history of the Jews in the reign of Caligula. Herod Agrippa was the brother of Herod Antipas' wife, Herodias, and he was a grandson of Herod the Great. He was something of a rake and a charmer. His father, Aristobulus, had been strangled on the command of Herod the Great, and Herod Agrippa went to Rome, where he came under the tutelage of Antonia. He fell heavily into debt in the capital, including an obligation of more than a million sesterces to Tiberius. Some time after AD 23 he returned to Judaea, and his sister, Herodias, persuaded her husband, Herod Antipas, to give him a small pension.

Herod Agrippa did not like anything small, and he soon quarrelled with his sister's husband. He went to Syria and took up residence with the Governor, Lucius Pomponius Flaccus, but was quickly involved in a scandal. He accepted a bribe to use his influence with the Governor in a court case and was expelled from Syria. Then he set out for Rome but was arrested along the way by a Procurator for the unpaid debt to Tiberius. Agrippa escaped, borrowed money at Alexandria, and arrived at Tiberius' residence on Capri in 36. Although the Emperor at first welcomed him warmly, a letter finally arrived from the Prefect, and Agrippa was barred from the Emperor's company. With typical brashness he borrowed the money he needed to repay Tiberius from his old friend, Antonia.

Back in the good graces of the Emperor, Agrippa stayed on Capri and became a good friend of the young Caligula. Then one of his servants accused him of treason with Caligula, and Macro arrested and imprisoned him, though no action was taken against the young Prince. After Tiberius died, Agrippa was soon released, and he resumed his friendship with the new, young Emperor. Caligula gave him the tetrarchy of Philip that had been annexed to Syria, as a kingdom, and he stayed in Rome enjoying the income of his new territory. In the summer of 38, after Drusilla's death, he returned to the East by way of Alexandria.

His sister, Herodias, was furious that her brother had been made King, while her husband, Herod Antipas, was merely a Tetrarch, so she cajoled him to go to Rome in 39 and ask Caligula for the title of King.[452] Agrippa sent a fast letter to Rome accusing Antipas of treason, and it was while Caligula was at Baiae that he received the message and confronted Antipas. Antipas and his wife were banished to Lyon, and Agrippa was given his territory.[453] In the summer of 40 Herod Agrippa was back in Rome, just in time to play an important role in a controversy involving Caligula and the Jews.

There was a large community of Jews living at this time in the city of Alexandria in Egypt. For the most part their relations with the Ptolemies had been good, but with the advent of Roman rule a serious division arose between Jews and Greeks in the city, perhaps caused by Jewish willingness to cooperate with the Romans, who were hated by the Greeks. Since the Greeks could not openly oppose Rome, they vented their frustrations against the Jews.[454]

Augustus had erected a bronze notice in Alexandria spelling out the religious and political rights of the Jews. Although there is no consensus among modern scholars about the exact nature of their rights, it is likely that they did not have citizenship in the city, but were organized under their own leaders, councils, and courts on matters of Jewish law,[455] maintaining an existence separate from the other local communities. They were allowed to gather on the Sabbath, though 'clubs' were normally prohibited in the Roman Empire as politically dangerous. They were also permitted to send annual contributions to the Temple in Jerusalem. One major concession made by Rome to the Jews everywhere was that they were not required to participate in the religious ceremonies held all over the Empire on the Emperor's birthday and other occasions; instead they were permitted to offer their own prayers for the Emperor's welfare in their places of worship. In Alexandria some individual Jews apparently tried, successfully, to get Alexandrian citizenship, because it brought exemption from one of the Roman taxes in Egypt. This complicated situation exacerbated relations between Greeks and Jews, as the Greeks resisted attempts to extend the citizenship to their Semitic neighbours.

Under Caligula there was a pogrom in the Jewish residential section of Alexandria.[456] There were five districts in Alexandria, one of which had legally been ceded to the Jews, although they had spread out into another as they grew in number. Some Jews even lived in other sections of the city. The Prefect of Egypt at the time was a man named Aulus Avillius Flaccus. He had been appointed by Tiberius late in 32 and was generally a popular governor. On the accession of Caligula Flaccus' position was jeopardized, and the new Emperor actually appointed Macro to succeed him, but Macro's death in 38 foreclosed that possibility. Flaccus stayed on in Egypt, but he was clearly a lame-duck Prefect, and out of concern for his personal position he quickly became ineffective. He seems to have forgotten to relay to Caesar the resolutions of congratulations the Jews of Alexandria had proposed for the Emperor on his accession.

Some Greek schemers suggested to the Governor that they would secure Greek support for retaining him in his office if he would yield to their desire to attack the Jews, probably by curtailing grants of citizenship to them and perhaps by reducing their privileges in the city. He agreed and began to show prejudice against the Jews in the courts. Naturally the Jews became alarmed, but the event that sparked serious trouble was the unexpected arrival of Herod Agrippa in Alexandria as he was returning east in August of 38 to assume the new kingship Caligula had given him.

Flaccus had not been told that Agrippa was coming, and the new King intended to arrive by night and slip away unnoticed. However, his presence in the city was discovered, and some Jews persuaded him to send the Emperor the message that Flaccus had failed to forward. Agrippa then decided to stay and help the Jews in their difficulties by parading through the streets of Alexandria with his bodyguard. Perhaps he hoped to indicate to the Governor that the Jews had a powerful friend in the imperial court, but Agrippa actually infuriated the Greeks. They staged a counter-demonstration and dressed up a local idiot in parody of the Jewish King. Flaccus decided to throw in his lot with the people who supported him, the Greeks, and he took no action to suppress their insults to the Jews.

The Greek activists seized the opportunity, and a mob spread throughout the city, occupying, burning and destroying Jewish synagogues and placing images of Caligula in some of them. Many Jews who lived outside the two Jewish districts retreated into them. Flaccus then issued a proclamation declaring the Jews aliens and requiring them to live within the one district that had originally been theirs. In the words of one eminent authority, this produced '. . . the first known ghetto in the world.'[457] The Greek mob hunted down Jews outside the Jewish district, chased some into the ghetto, and cruelly tortured and killed others. There was extensive looting, and a plague broke out in the overcrowded ghetto. Unemployment and poverty crippled many. Because of food shortages some Jews went out into the Gentile markets and were lynched. On the Emperor's birthday, 31 August, thirty-eight members of the Jewish Senate were openly whipped in the theatre. Greeks forced Jewish women to eat pork in public.

In the uneasy calm that followed the pogrom, troops arrived from Rome to arrest Flaccus. The new Prefect, Gaius Vitrasius Pollio, was wiser than Flaccus, and he allowed the Jews to return to their earlier districts and resume their professions. The question of their legal status was referred to the Emperor, and both the Greeks and the Jews sent delegations to Italy to plead their cases. Two points were in dispute. One was the right of the Jews to practise their religion (including the exemption from celebrating the Emperor's birthday), and the other was their civic rights in Alexandria. Leader of the Jewish delegation was Philo Judaeus, whose accounts of these matters constitute our major ancient source. In the winter of 39–40 they set sail and probably arrived while Caligula was still in the North.[458]

When the Emperor returned from Gaul, he met briefly with both delegations. In the Gardens of Agrippina outside Rome Caligula cordially told the Jews he would see them again later. In fact, it was several months before they got their promised audience with the Emperor, and in the interval something much more important happened to upset them – the Emperor ordered his statue to be set up in the Temple at Jerusalem.[459]

The Roman Procurator at Jamnia in Judaea, a man named Herennius Capito, the same person who had arrested Herod Agrippa for the debt he owed Tiberius, reported early in AD 40 to Caligula that Gentiles in the city had set up an altar to the Emperor.[460] The Jews had torn it down. The angry and increasingly insane Caesar decided to teach them a lesson. He ordered Publius Petronius, the Governor of Syria, to construct a huge statue of the Emperor dressed as Jupiter and to use two of the four legions of his province to escort it to Jerusalem, employing force if necessary to place it in the Holy of Holies, the inner sanctuary of the Temple.[461] Under Jewish law no one but the High Priest could enter the inner sanctuary of the Temple, and then only on the Day of Atonement.

Caligula intended to make even the Jews worship him as a god. Petronius was a good and courageous Governor, and he knew that this order would cause rebellion and suffering in Judaea, so he delayed as long as possible. The statue was being made in Sidon, and Petronius may have ordered one so elaborate that it could not be prepared quickly. While awaiting the construction of the image, the Governor met with Jewish leaders and tried to persuade them to acquiesce in the Emperor's orders, but they made it clear that the presence of an imperial statue in the Temple was simply unacceptable.

In May 40 Petronius moved south with his legions. At Ptolemais on the border of Galilee, a crowd of Jews, some of whom had come from as far away as Jerusalem, opposed his advance. The Jews would not tolerate the desecration of their temple. Petronius sent orders to the workmen in Sidon not to rush completion of the statue, then left his military forces at Ptolemais and proceeded to Tiberias in Galilee, the capital of Herod Antipas, who had left for Italy on his own hopeless mission. At Tiberias a delegation of Jewish leaders urged him to write to Caligula, and Petronius decided to do so, despite the risks.

The letter he sent to the Emperor explained the delay in carrying out the orders. The Jews were so upset by the threat to their temple that they were neglecting the fields and the harvest was in danger. Considering the fact that the Emperor had announced his intention of visiting Egypt in the near future, Petronius wondered whether a famine in the East might not be a great inconvenience to the imperial party. Also a Jewish revolt represented a loss in imperial revenues. Petronius seems to have laid out the dilemma for the Emperor in a skilful fashion, tactfully pointing out the dangers and asking Caligula to reconsider.

Naturally this merely angered the impatient Caesar, who believed that Petronius had been bribed, but he composed a restrained reply, ordering the Governor to proceed with the installation of the statue, since the crops would by now be in (it was probably the late summer of 40). Petronius, however, continued to delay, and eventually was rewarded for his wisdom.

In the meantime, Herod Agrippa, who did have a close relationship with Caligula, had returned to Rome, ignorant of what the Emperor had commanded. When he heard about it, he was very shocked and possibly suffered a stroke.[462] Upon recovery he composed a long, well-documented letter to Caligula reminding him of imperial policy towards the Jews.[463] Out of friendship for Agrippa, the Emperor changed his mind and countermanded his order to Petronius.[464] The ruler stipulated, however, that in the future the Jews should not interfere with Gentile efforts to introduce the imperial cult in areas outside Jerusalem.

According to Philo, Caligula reneged on his deal and tried once again to place his statue in the Temple; at least he planned to build a statue in Rome, secretly, and take it with him on his trip to the East. He hoped to catch the Jews by surprise and install the image before they could gather the strength to oppose it. Fortunately, if the story is true, Caligula died before he could actually carry out this plan. No Emperor had ever gone so far in offending the Jews, and Claudius soon reaffirmed their traditional rights, criticizing Caligula's 'madness' in the process. Another grim story in the reign of Caligula had come to an end. This one might have produced a genuine catastrophe, had not time and fate intervened.

10. Caligula and the Provinces

In a biography of almost any other Roman Emperor this chapter would have been entitled 'The Provincial Policy of. . . .', but Caligula was much too erratic for the use of that expression. One recent biographer has professed to see 'no consistency or coherence in his policies', which is to say that he had none, in the normal sense of the word.[465] Certainly he had no provincial policy, despite the Herculean effort of some modern historians to deduce one for him. He used the provinces as sources of revenue, as playthings for his amusement, and as rewards for his friends.

We have already seen how Caligula rewarded Herod Agrippa with significant possessions in the East, and how the Emperor behaved on his trip to the northern frontier. North Africa also provided opportunities for his amusement. Much of the North African coast had been under Roman rule since the days of the Carthaginian Wars. What the Romans called the province of Africa was actually roughly the modern nation of Tunisia. To the west, in modern Algeria, lay in ancient times the kingdom of Numidia, whose last king, Juba I, committed suicide after Julius Caesar defeated the Pompeians in North Africa in 46 BC. Augustus combined Numidia with the province of Africa. To the east, the modern Libya was the province of Cyrene.[466]

In imperial times the province of Africa was populous and wealthy, one of the few provinces governed by a Proconsul selected at least formally by the Senate, who had a legion under his personal command. After the death of Augustus Africa was the only province with a legion not officially under the Emperor's control.

West of Africa was Mauretania, organized as a client kingdom or satellite state by the Emperor Augustus. He placed a king on the throne, Juba's son, Juba II, and allowed Juba II to marry Cleopatra Selene, a daughter of Antony and Cleopatra. Though urbane and sophisticated, Juba proved singularly incompetent. On his death in 23 his son Ptolemy succeeded to the throne, but he was a tyrant whose subjects rose up against him, although the rebellion was suppressed by Roman forces under the Governor of Africa. On the occasion of Ptolemy's 'victory', he was awarded by the Senate an ivory sceptre and a purple toga decorated with gold stars.[467]

King Ptolemy of Mauretania then graciously drops from the pages of history from AD 24 until his reappearance in the reign of Caligula. What we are told by the ancient sources is that the Emperor executed him in 40, probably after his return from the North.[468] As inevitably happens when a despot acts whimsically, there are two versions of his supposed crime. Dio claims that Caligula persecuted Ptolemy because he was wealthy, and Suetonius says that Ptolemy had angered Caligula by appearing at a public event wearing a purple cloak. Under Augustus foreign kings wore only a plain toga in the Emperor's presence, but Tiberius had abandoned the practice.[469]

Modern historians have struggled mightily to rationalize Caligula's action. Two explanations have met with considerable support. One is that it made sense strategically to annex Mauretania as a province (which is what ultimately happened) and the other is that Ptolemy was somehow involved in the conspiracy of Lepidus and Gaetulicus.[470] There is no shred of ancient evidence for either theory. It is true that the elimination of the client kingdoms and the incorporation of their territory directly under Roman rule made strategic sense and had actually happened by the end of the first century. Caligula was not exactly one of Rome's greatest strategic thinkers, however, and his favours to the client kings of the East reflect none of the strategic wisdom of Vespasian, who simply eliminated most of them (though he did not kill them).

As for the connection with the conspiracy of Lepidus and

Gaetulicus, only a tiny and relatively insignificant thread links Ptolemy with them. He was related to Caligula's sisters, since he was a grandson of Mark Antony. Possibly, it has been suggested, this family connection drew him into the web of treason. On the other hand, he was also related to Caligula, but the important point is that we have no knowledge and no reason to believe that he had spent any time with his relatives in Rome. Another argument is that Gaetulicus' father had fought as comrade-in-arms with Juba II, Ptolemy's father. That is much too weak a reed to support a conspiracy theory, lacking any other evidence. It is true, as some have observed, that execution was a severe penalty for Ptolemy's 'crimes', but Caligula was certainly cruel and also arbitrary. There is no need to 'make sense' of this story; it is merely another of many examples of the Emperor's insane jealousy and greed, qualities that reinforced one another in this case.

The incorporation of Mauretania as a province did prove advantageous, although the immediate effect was the outbreak of a revolt against Roman authority by the natives under a leader named Aedemon. After the suppression of this rebellion Mauretania was divided into two provinces, Mauretania Tingitana and Mauretania Caesariensis. According to Pliny, Caligula was responsible for the division, and according to Dio it was Claudius. The preponderance of evidence actually favours Claudius.[471]

Caligula did, however, make one change in the administration of the African provinces. He took control of the legion in the province of Africa from its senatorial governor and placed it in the hands of an imperial legate. Although that too made administrative sense, because the Emperor was elsewhere responsible for the defence of the Empire, Tacitus and Dio say that Caligula's reason was his fear of the Governor of Africa, but they name different men.[472] Despite the confusion of names, they must have hit on the truth. One recent authority has said, 'There is no reason to question that Caligula's action was a sound one, dictated by a sober evaluation of the circumstances, rather than by fear or hatred, as Dio and Tacitus suggest.'[473] On the contrary, I think there is every reason to doubt that Caligula acted on a 'sober evaluation of the circumstances'. There is some question as to how often Caligula was actually sober, but alcoholism aside, the Emperor showed so little good judgment that Tacitus and Dio may be confidently trusted on this point.[474]

Equally in the East Caligula's actions reflect whimsy rather than policy. The Emperor Augustus, after defeating Antony and Cleopatra, had inherited a system of client kings in the East, a system that had developed in the days of the Late Roman Republic and was further modified by Antony during his long reign there. Syria, Judaea and Egypt were all provinces of the Roman Empire by the death of Augustus, and we have already seen how Caligula advanced the interests of his friend, Herod Agrippa, among the Jews.

For the most part the client kings were an anomaly in the Roman Empire. In his famous study of Roman grand strategy Edward Luttwak argues that the Julio-Claudians wisely used the client kings to reduce the costs of defence while they pursued a flexible grand strategy around the Empire.[475] According to him, the client kings served a useful military role in Rome's overall defence plan. I believe this is not the case.[476] From Augustus' time onward, after the defeat in the Teutoburg Forest, Augustus and Tiberius regarded the Rhine and the Danube as the frontier of the Empire, and legions were permanently stationed along that line. They did not yet enjoy the great stone fortresses and walls that characterize the grand strategy of preclusive security so obviously in place by the reign of Hadrian in the second century, but the basic strategy of deploying all available manpower around a well-defined defensive perimeter was clearly emerging even under Augustus.

The client kings, then, should be regarded as a temporary expedient, dictated by political rather than by military considerations. After the victory at Actium Augustus had his hands full reorganizing the Empire, and he decided to leave the political organization in the East much as he had found it, though he had to modify all the concessions Antony had granted to Cleopatra in the region. But the puppet states were doomed from the beginning. Roman legions were capable of defending the Empire, and the emperors were generally unwilling to tolerate militarily powerful local princes on the margins. Augustus himself eventually transformed Judaea into a province, and Tiberius annexed Cappadocia and Commagene.

Caligula's impact on Roman foreign and military policy was catastrophic, far worse than his modern biographers have realized. Despite his ridiculous campaign in the North in 39 and 40, he firmly planted the idea of Roman conquest of Britain. That was extraordinarily unwise. Conceived by a mad man (Caligula) and executed by a fool (Claudius), the conquest of Britain, obviously rejected by the much better strategists, Augustus and Tiberius, proved a permanent drain on Roman military manpower, since there were three legions, and sometimes four, attached to the province. There were by the second century A D twenty-nine or thirty legions, and Britain needed ten per cent of Rome's standing forces. The contributions of Britain to Roman civilization were minimal compared with those of Gaul and Spain, and the military threat to the Empire from the Celts of Britain was negligible.[477] Caligula and Claudius left a burdensome heritage.

Caligula's eastern activities (it is difficult to call them policies) also attest to his folly. The major threat in the East was from Parthia, and late in the reign of Tiberius the Parthian king, Artabanus, had pursued provocative policies. But Vitellius, the Governor of Syria (who later introduced prostration to the court of Caligula) made a show of force, and when the young Caesar succeeded Tiberius, Artabanus met Vitellius on the Euphrates and called off hostilities.[478] Actually internal unrest in Parthia precluded any serious threat to Rome while Caligula was Emperor.

The main bone of contention between Rome and Parthia had been control over Armenia. Because of Armenia's strategic location, Roman control in the region provided a base for an attack against Parthia's flank in the event she launched an invasion of Rome's eastern territories. It was also true that Armenia might serve as a convenient launching point for a Roman invasion of Parthia. Although there had been problems with Parthia in the reigns of Augustus and Tiberius, the main line of policy was for Rome to have a friendly king on the Armenian throne. When Caligula came to power, the Armenian king was Mithridates. He had been helped to the throne by the Romans under Tiberius.

At the beginning of Caligula's reign the Emperor called Mithridates to Rome and put him in prison.[479] Ancient authors give no reason for Caesar's action, but for the rest of his reign Rome had no candidate on the Armenian throne. Control of Armenia had been a major feature of Roman policy in the East, and it would continue to be afterwards. Caligula's successor, Claudius, early in his reign, restored Mithridates to the throne.[480] Caligula's neglect of the situation in Armenia led to no great problem, but the argument from silence – that Caligula successfully pursued a policy of peace – is utter nonsense.[481]

Elsewhere in the East Caligula made equally serious mistakes, driven by purely personal considerations. When he was living with Antonia in his teens, he had become friends with three Thracian princes. Their father, Cotys, had once been king of part of Thrace while his brother, Rhescuporis, ruled the rest. When Rhescuporis killed Cotys, Tiberius deposed the surviving murderer and named the son of Rhescuporis king in his father's place, and the three young sons of Cotys – Rhoemetalces, Polemo and Cotys II – kings in their father's stead. Since they were infants, Tiberius brought them to Rome and sent a regent to govern their joint kingdom.

When Caligula became Rome's ruler, he rewarded his three friends far more richly than they had ever been promised.[482] At a ceremony in the Forum (probably some time in 38), the Emperor, sitting on the rostra on a chair between the consuls, protected from the sun by silken awnings, proclaimed Rhoemetalces king of his ancestral territory in Thrace. Polemo, whose connection with Caligula may have been strengthened by his marriage to Herod Agrippa's sister, Berenice, was named king of Pontus and the Bosphorus. Cotys was allocated Armenia Minor.[483]

A recent biographer has said:

In fact, Caligula seems to have achieved some of his greatest successes in his dealings with the client-kings, and in his arrangements for the eastern part of the empire was able to display the most creative application of his autocratic powers. Caligula seems to have been concerned primarily with preserving stability in this part of his empire, rather than with extending the Roman imperium . . . and client rulers were an excellent means to this end.[484]

On the contrary, Caligula created new client kingdoms when the strategic and political need, as well as the trend, was to reduce them; and the lavish gifts of territory to his friends were certainly personal and not a matter of policy. The Empire was strong enough to withstand such nonsense, and by the end of the century the client kings were gone, but Caligula retarded rather than accelerated the process. His most extravagant act was to place Antiochus IV back on the throne of Commagene, which had been a Roman province since the death of his father Antiochus III in AD 17.[485] In addition Caligula gave Antiochus IV part of Cilicia, but what is worse, considering the Emperor's financial problems, was that Antiochus IV received the staggering sum of one hundred million sesterces, perhaps twenty-five per cent of the annual revenues of the Roman Empire, because that was the amount Rome had received from the area as a province.[486] This perverted generosity had its limits. For some unknown reason Caligula later deposed Antiochus IV, who was eventually reinstated by Claudius.

It has been suggested that Caligula used client kings because he did not trust Roman senators to govern the provinces, but there probably is not even that much policy behind the Emperor's moves. Whimsy, caprice, personal friendships and personal animosities were the driving factors in his relations with the client kings, just as they were in most of his actions.

11. *Murder and Godlessness*

Suetonius' biography of Caligula in *The Lives of the Twelve Caesars* begins with a few items illustrating positive features of the reign, but then the ancient biographer in a famous passage stops abruptly and writes, 'So much for the prince – now for the monster.'[487] Suetonius proceeds to relate all the unpleasant stories we have reviewed in this book. Twentieth-century scholars have struggled to rationalize many of these stories to make Caligula appear better than he actually was. It would be worthwhile to look closely at the so-called 'good' policies Suetonius attributes to Caligula in the brief section on the 'prince' as opposed to the 'monster'.

He begins by telling of the joy of the Roman people who finally had a popular young Emperor. There were many games and celebrations. When Caligula fell ill, the whole world prayed for his recovery. The Emperor collected the ashes of members of his family and brought them to Rome amid great enthusiasm. He named the month of September after his father, Germanicus, and he adopted Tiberius Gemellus. His sisters were included in the imperial oaths, and he recalled all exiles, promising that there would be no further prosecutions. The new Caesar banished sexual perverts from the city and removed literary censorship. He transferred elections to the people, published the imperial budget, paid the legacies bequeathed by Tiberius, and even those earlier bequeathed by Tiberius' mother, Livia, which Tiberius had not paid. He reduced taxes.

Suetonius also says that whenever he restored kings to their thrones he paid the back revenues that had accrued. He rewarded a freedwoman with a gift of eight hundred thousand sesterces because she had not implicated her former master in a crime, even under torture. He held four consulships. He twice gave the people gifts of three hundred sesterces each, provided banquets and presents for senators and equestrians, and added a day to the Saturnalia to extend the holiday season. He gave many gladiatorial shows and dramatic performances. He promoted a senator to the praetorship ahead of his regular time. He provided a splendid pageant when he bridged the gulf between Puteoli and Baiae, and he sponsored games in the provinces also. He finished some public building projects that had begun under Tiberius and began construction of an aqueduct and amphitheatre. Caligula also repaired the walls of Syracuse and rebuilt some temples. He even planned to dig a canal at the Isthmus of Corinth and actually sent a surveyor to the site.

So much for the prince. On close examination the list adds up to very little. Caligula transferred the elections back to the Senate before his reign was over. His relations with the client kings were personal and extravagant, and they ran counter to the trend of the first century. The Emperor lost his popularity with the Senate and the people relatively quickly. He rebuilt the theatre of Pompey the Great, which had been destroyed by fire and partially restored under Tiberius, but removed the names of both Pompey and Tiberius from the structure. Claudius later added them.[488] In addition Caligula required Gnaeus Pompeius Magnus, a descendant through his mother of Pompey the Great, to stop using the name 'Magnus', and considered killing him, saying that it was not safe to have anyone styled 'the Great', but Claudius restored the title and allowed Pompeius to marry his daughter, Antonia.[489]

Although the Emperor promised to end the treason trials, they became a notorious feature of his reign. Even his sisters, who were originally included in the oaths, were sent into banishment under humiliating conditions. He murdered Tiberius Gemellus after adopting him. The banishment of sexual perverts hardly seems commendable considering the Emperor's own sexual proclivities. His fiscal policies and extravagant generosity led to bankruptcy, and despite the initial popularity of the games, the people and the Senate became dissatisfied with them too. In short, there is nothing in Suetonius' list of the 'prince's' actions that does not recur in a perverted form under the 'monster'. Caligula did not have two personalities, one good and one bad. He was simply crazy, and there were times when his insanity did not manifest itself in cruelty, vainglory or extravagance. On occasion he was even charming, as criminally insane people can be even today.

Nor was he an idiot. Had he been, he would never have become Emperor of Rome. He sometimes exhibited a crafty intellect, which does not mean that he was intelligent. If he had not been Emperor of Rome, he might have been merely peculiar, possibly an eccentric. But imperial power, undefined and nearly limitless, was too great a burden for his sick and troubled mind to bear. It did indeed often make him a monster, and occasionally he was simply comical. Cruelty, megalomania, recklessness, and rapacity characterize his personality and his reign. Under the circumstances it is surprising that he ruled for so long, although Rome had at least two other terrible Emperors, Nero and Commodus, who ruled for much longer.

Barrett has argued that in his 'private pursuits' Caligula was 'no better, but no worse, than his peers'.[490] Even if that were true, it would be a left-handed compliment, considering that Caligula's peers were Tiberius, Claudius, and Nero. But in fact Caligula was far and away the worst of all. In the first place each of the others had some reasonably redeeming features, but Caligula's reign is almost entirely without positive achievement. Setting that aside, the young Emperor, who had far fewer years of rule to make his mark than the other three, really has no peers in personal peculiarities. In addition to the women he seduced, the list of his male lovers is impressive. One was Lepidus, another was the actor Mnester, and there is a famous story about his affair with a senatorial aristocrat named Valerius Catullus. Catullus boasted publicly that he had buggered the Emperor and that he had worn himself out doing it.[491]

One of his crazes was for pageantry and the games. His gladiatorial shows were spectacular by earlier standards, and he was personally acquainted with many gladiators, some of whom accompanied him on the campaign in the North. In Rome the Emperor was a supporter of the Thracian gladiators, who used small, round shields. Their opponents were the *murmillones*, armed with the larger oblong shields. Probably to make things easier for his favoured Thracians the Emperor ordered a reduction in the amount of armour the *murmillones* could wear, and when one of them, Columbus, won a fight, he had poison rubbed on the victor's wounds, afterwards referring to it as 'Columbinum'.[492] Caligula sometimes took part in the combats himself, though no gladiator dared harm him. In a mock contest against a *murmillo* with a wooden sword, his opponent tactfully stumbled before the Emperor. Caligula stabbed him with a real dagger and then paraded around with a palm branch, the way winners did.[493] He forced other men of rank to compete in the arena as well.

The Emperor had a knack for unusual ways of making money, and he used the games for that purpose. After the fights he sold the victors at auction, forcing the two Praetors who were responsible for the games to buy them, himself bidding up the prices to grossly inflated levels. Sycophants came to these auctions to help the Emperor, either by buying or by raising the bids.[494] A certain Aponius Saturninus made the mistake of falling asleep at one of the sales, and Caligula told the auctioneer to pay attention to the nodding gentleman. When he awoke, he found that he had purchased thirteen gladiators at a price of nine million sesterces![495]

Nothing was as important to Caligula, however, as the horse-races. He had his own horses, and he built a track for them, called the *Gaianum*, on his property on the Vatican across the Tiber.[496] Today St Peter's Cathedral covers some of the site, and the obelisk that Caligula transported from Egypt for his new track is still there, though it was relocated in 1586.[497] In horse-racing Caligula was a partisan of the Greens, and he is supposed to have poisoned the horses and the drivers of the Blues.[498] The Emperor sometimes drove the chariots himself, and he occasionally dined with the Greens and offered them gifts. One of the drivers, Eutychus, received two million sesterces.[499]

Probably the best-known story about Caligula is that he had a favourite horse, Incitatus, kept in a fabulous stable with a marble stall and an ivory manger. The horse had purple blankets, a collar with gems, and its own servants. Caligula invited this horse to dinner and toasted him from golden goblets. On the day before the races Caligula sent soldiers through the neighbourhood ordering silence, so Incitatus could get his rest. The Emperor sometimes swore by the animal's life and fortune.[500] The number of horse-races increased dramatically under Caligula, and senators, who had been forbidden to participate under Tiberius, drove chariots over sand mixed with red and green colouring.[501] Naturally Caligula's passion for racing was popular with the crowd at the track, but Romans of probity and restraint recoiled in shock.

Caligula's reign came to an abrupt end on 24 January AD 41.[502] It was only three years and nine months since his joyful accession. Significantly the conspiracy that led to his assassination grew up in the circle of his own closest associates. One of them was a former slave, Callistus, who was phenomenally wealthy and influential at court.[503] He remained prominent under Claudius. Former slaves of the imperial family, the so-called freedmen, often had considerable authority because of the close personal relationship they had with their masters as former slaves. Under Claudius several freedmen gained excessive influence at court and in the management of the Empire generally.

In addition to Callistus the two Prefects of the Praetorian Guard joined the conspiracy.[504] One of them was Marcus Arrecinus Clemens, but the name of the other is unknown.[505] By far the most important conspirator was a tribune of the Praetorian Guard, a man named Cassius Chaerea. He was appalled at the unbridled absolutism of Caligula's regime, and he had a personal score to settle with the Emperor. He spoke in a high-pitched, effeminate voice, though he was otherwise strong and manly, and the Emperor constantly made fun of him. He called the man a 'girl', and since the Tribune had to ask Caligula personally for the password each day, the Emperor taunted him by choosing words with sexual connotations, such as 'Venus' or 'Priapus'. He made obscene gestures to Chaerea, and the Praetorians began to laugh at their Tribune. According to Seneca, Caligula drove Chaerea to use the sword so as not to have to get the password.[506]

Still, there was enough discontent with the Emperor that Chaerea succeeded in recruiting some of the other Tribunes to join in the conspiracy. One was named Papinius and another Cornelius Sabinus.[507] Several distinguished senators were also members, including Lucius Annius Vinicianus, who had been a friend of Lepidus.[508] Another major figure was Valerius Asiaticus, who was closely associated with Antonia. Caligula had embarrassed the famous senator by teasing him in the presence of others about his wife's lacklustre performance in bed.[509] Later Asiaticus lost his life, a victim of Claudius' wife, Messalina.[510] The historian Cluvius Rufus, an ex-consul whose work unfortunately has not survived, also joined the conspirators.[511] Two other senators known to have been involved were Publius Nonius Asprenas and Lucius Norbanus Balbus, but undoubtedly there were some whose names have not survived.[512] Naturally, the password for the conspiracy was '*Libertas*'.

The conspirators decided to act on 24 January, the last day of the Palatine Games.[513] There would be a large crowd jammed into a makeshift structure near the Emperor's palace. The imperial bodyguard would have little room to help Caligula fend off his assassins, and, besides, there was a rumour that the Emperor planned to leave Rome immediately after the games for Alexandria, so the conspirators realized that time was short.[514] The ancient sources relate a number of omens that foretold the Emperor's death, although Caligula did not take any notice of them. He had ordered the Governor of Achaea to dismantle the statue of Zeus at Olympia and ship it to Rome, but it burst out laughing and scared the workers away. Caligula himself had a dream the night before that Jupiter had kicked him out of heaven (with his left foot). Even the presentations on the last day of the games were ominous. One was the *Cinyras*, a dancing drama in which the hero and his daughter were killed, in great violence mingled with incest. Another was called the *Laureolus*. In it the leading actor was required to stumble and vomit blood. After the performance was over the understudies competed with one another in the role, and the stage was literally covered with blood.[515]

Caligula arrived at the theatre in the morning. He was in good spirits, and there was already a large crowd. The confusion of the mob seemed to amuse him, and when he sacrificed a flamingo to Augustus, the blood spurted out on him and possibly on some bystanders.[516] Then the Emperor took his seat and began to eat and drink, along with his companions. The consul Pomponius Secundus was among them, eating, drinking, and kissing the Emperor's feet.[517] As a general rule, Caligula left the games at lunch-time, and the conspirators planned to kill him as he walked back through a narrow passage to the palace. For some reason, however, on that day Caligula delayed his lunch. Chaerea was anxious and headed for the exit the Emperor would take. Vinicianus got up to encourage Chaerea to do the deed, but Caligula asked him where he was going, so he sat down again. Then at around one o'clock the senator Asprenas persuaded the Emperor to leave, just as Chaerea was about to kill him in the open. When the imperial retinue retired, the crowd was kept at bay, so there would be no one nearby to help Caligula.[518]

The Emperor decided to go by a different route, and that was fortunate for the conspirators, because the one taken by the other members of his party had guards. On his way through the unguarded passage to the palace, Caligula stopped to visit some young Asian actors who were rehearsing for their performance, and the conspirators decided to strike.[519] There are different versions of what happened at this point, but the differences are minor and insignificant. Chaerea struck the first blow, cutting the Emperor between the neck and shoulder, according to one account, driving his sword through Caligula's jaw, according to another.[520] Another Praetorian Tribune, Sabinus, then delivered a second blow that knocked the Emperor down, and the remaining conspirators fell on him, stabbing him some thirty times. Suetonius reports that some of the assassins ran their weapons through the Emperor's private parts, and Dio Cassius adds that a few even ate Caligula's flesh.[521]

There were some who tried to defend the Emperor. His litter-bearers attacked the conspirators, and they fled into the part of the palace known as the House of Germanicus.[522] Caligula's German bodyguard reacted in frenzy and killed Asprenas and Norbanus Balbus. A number of innocent people in the general vicinity also fell victims to the Germans, as well as one conspirator who could not resist looking at Caligula's dead body for the sheer pleasure of it. As the Germans closed off entry and exit to the area, some of them dumped the heads of their victims onto the altar of Augustus.[523] Naturally in such a crisis, there were many rumours – Caligula was alive; he had escaped; he had actually made up the story to see how loyal the people would be to him.[524] There was also a rumour that he had planned to make his horse Consul of the Roman People.[525]

The conspirators were not through with their bloody work. A Praetorian Tribune was sent to kill Caligula's wife, Caesonia. She was found crying over his body, stained with his blood, and her little daughter, Drusilla, was with her. Caesonia fell to the Tribune's sword, and a soldier picked up the child, Drusilla, by her feet and bashed her brains out against the wall.[526]

The present chapter is entitled 'Murder and Godlessness' because of a comment made by the historian, Dio Cassius, that on this day Caligula 'learned by actual experience that he was not a god'.[527]

Epilogue

On the day Caligula was assassinated, his friend Herod Agrippa was still in Rome. During his lifetime the Emperor had been criticized for having such close personal relations with Agrippa and the other client kings. They were called his 'tutors in tyranny', but Agrippa at least remained a true friend.[528] He made arrangements in the afternoon of the fateful day to provide for Caligula's remains. The body was taken to the Lamian Gardens on the Esquiline. There Agrippa, acting quickly, made sure that it was partially cremated, and the charred body was buried in a shallow grave. When the dead Emperor's sisters returned from exile, they exhumed what was left of the body, cremated it, and placed the ashes in a tomb, possibly in the mausoleum of Augustus, but the exact location is unknown.

Caretakers at the Lamian Gardens complained that they had been haunted by ghosts because of the Emperor's burial there. Caligula's spirit also haunted the part of the palace where he had died; according to Suetonius, there was not a night there without some frightening event. The Emperor's ghostly spectre cursed the area until the palace was finally destroyed by fire nearly forty years later.[529] He was the first Roman Emperor who did not receive a state funeral.

Caligula's legacy to Rome was trivial. He left little to his subjects that was lasting and important. There were a few construction projects and administrative decisions, but on the negative side, his scores were much higher. He had squandered the splendid opportunity that his father's popularity had given him at the outset of his reign. His capricious tyranny would surely have provoked civil war if he had remained on the throne, and Judaea was nearly in rebellion when he died. His main contribution, if it can be called that, was to the growing autocracy of the emperorship. Some of the rumours about him that have survived may not be true, but the fact that they circulated widely indicates what his fellow Romans thought of him and constitutes a damning verdict in the court of history. Rarely has so little good been done by so powerful a figure, and there are only a few rulers in all the history of the world who were as crazy, cruel, conceited, and arbitrary as the Roman Emperor, Caligula.

Select Bibliography

This bibliography contains only those items cited in the notes in a shortened form (e.g., Balsdon 1934). Articles in classical journals have generally been cited in full in the notes and are not included here.

Aalders, G.J.D., *Caligula, zoon van Germanicus*, Assen 1959.

Akveld, W.F., *Germanicus*, Groningen 1961.

Alfoldy, G., *Noricum*, London 1974.

Applebaum, Shimon, *Judaea in Hellenistic and Roman Times*, Leiden 1989.

Auguet, Roland, *Caligula, ou le pouvoir à vingt ans*, Paris 1975.

Badian, Ernst, *Publicans and Sinners*, Ithaca 1972.

Baldwin, Barry, *The Roman Emperors*, Montreal 1980.

Balsdon, J.P.V.D., *The Emperor Gaius (Caligula)*, Oxford 1934, several times reprinted.

Barrett, Anthony A., *Caligula: The Corruption of Power*, London 1989.

Bauman, R.A., *Impietas in Principem*, Munich 1974.

Bellen, Heinz, *Die germanische Leibwache der römischen Kaiser des julisch-claudischen Hauses*, Mainz 1981.

Bengtson, H., *Marcus Antonius*, Munich 1977.

—, *Kaiser Augustus*, Munich 1981.

Bogue, J.F., *Tiberius in the Reign of Augustus*, University of Illinois doctoral dissertation 1970.

Braund, David C., *Augustus to Nero: A Sourcebook on Roman history 31 BC–AD 68*, Totowa 1985.

—, *Rome and the Friendly King*, London 1984.

Brogan, Olwen, *Roman Gaul*, Harvard and London 1953.

Broughton, T.R.S., *The Romanization of Africa Proconsularis*, New York 1968.

Camus, Albert, *Caligula and 3 other plays*, New York 1958 (trans. Stuart Gilbert).

Carettoni, Gianfilippo, *Das Haus des Augustus auf dem Palatin*, Mainz 1983.

Carter, John M., *The Battle of Actium*, London 1970.

Colledge, M.A.R., *The Parthians*, London and New York 1967.

Cook, David A., *A History of Narrative Film*, London and New York 1981.

Cooke, Alistair, *Masterpieces: a Decade of Masterpiece Theatre*, New York 1981.

Cramer, Frederick H., *Astrology in Roman law and politics*, Philadelphia 1954.

D'Arms, John H., *Romans on the Bay of Naples*, Cambridge, Mass. 1970.

Deroux, Carl, *Studies in Latin Literature and Roman History, II*, Collection Latomus, vol. 168, Brussels 1980.

Dio Cassius, *Dio's Roman History* (trans. E. Cary), Loeb Library 1924.

Doumet, Joseph, *Étude sur la couleur pourpre ancienne*, Beirut 1980.

Drinkwater, J.F., *Roman Gaul*, London 1983.

Dudley, D.R., and Webster, G., *The Roman Conquest of Britain*, London 1965.

Durry, Marcel, *Les cohortes prétoriennes*, Paris 1938.

Eadie, John, and Ober, Josiah, ed., *The Craft of the Ancient Historian: Essays in Honor of Chester G. Starr*, Lanham, Maryland, 1985.

Earl, D.C., *The Age of Augustus*, London and New York 1968.

Eck, Werner, *Die Statthalter der germanischen Provinzen vom 1.–3. Jahrhundert*, Bonn 1985.

Ennen, Edith, *The Medieval Town*, New York 1979.

Feldman, Louis H., and Hata, Gohei, *Josephus, Judaism, and Christianity*, Detroit 1987.

—, *Josephus, the Bible, and History*, Detroit 1989.

Fentress, E.W.B., *Numidia and the Roman Army*, Oxford 1979.

Ferguson, W.S., *Hellenistic Athens*, London 1911.

Ferrill, Arther, *Seneca: The Rise to Power*, University of Illinois doctoral dissertation 1964.

—, *The Emperor Augustus: From Republic to Empire*, St. Louis 1978.

—, *The Fall of the Roman Empire: The Military Explanation*, London and New York 1986.

—, *Roman Imperial Grand Strategy*, Lanham, Maryland 1991.

Freis, Helmut, *Die cohortes urbanae*, Cologne 1967.

Frend, W.H.C., *The Rise of Christianity*, London 1984.

Frere, S.S., *Britannia: a History of Roman Britain*, 3rd ed., London 1987.

Frier, B., *Landlords and Tenants in Imperial Rome*, Princeton 1980.

Fuller, J.F.C., *Julius Caesar: Man, Soldier, and Tyrant*, London, 1965.

Garnsey, Peter, and Saller, Richard, *The Roman Empire*, Berkeley 1987.

Garzetti, Albino, *From Tiberius to the Antonines*, London 1974.

Gelzer, M., *Caesar: Politician and Statesman*, Oxford 1968.

Goodenough, Edwin R., *The Jurisprudence of the Jewish Courts in Egypt*, Amsterdam 1968.

Goodman, Martin, *The Ruling Class of Judaea*, London 1987.

Grant, Michael, *Cleopatra*, New York 1972.

—, *Caesar*, Chicago 1975.

Grenade, Pierre, *Essai sur les origines du principat*, Paris 1961.

Griffin, Miriam, *Seneca: A Philosopher in Politics*, Oxford 1976.

—, *Nero: The End of a Dynasty*, London 1984.

Grimal, P., *Les jardins romains à la fin de la République et aux deux premiers siècles de l'Empire*, 3rd ed., Paris 1984.

Hallett, Judith, *Fathers and Daughters in Roman Society*, Princeton 1984.

Hammond, Mason, *The Augustan Principate*, Cambridge, Mass. 1933.

Hammond, M., *The City in the Ancient World*, Harvard 1972.

Hammond, N.G.L., and Scullard, H.H., *Oxford Classical Dictionary*, 2nd ed., Oxford 1970.

Hanson, W., and Maxwell, G., *Rome's North-west Frontier*, Edinburgh 1983.

Hartley, B., and Wacher, J., *Rome and Her Northern Provinces*, Gloucester 1983.

Hennig, D., *L. Aelius Seianus*, Munich 1975.

Hermann, P., *Der römische Kaisereid*, Göttingen 1968.

Hoddinott, R.F., *Bulgaria in Antiquity*, London 1975.

Humphrey, J.W., *An Historical Commentary on Cassius Dio's Roman History, Book 59 (Gaius Caligula)*, Vancouver 1976 (University of British Columbia dissertation).

Huzar, Eleanor, *Mark Antony: A Biography*, Minneapolis 1978.

Jerome, T.S., *Aspects of the Study of Roman History*, New York 1962 (originally published in 1923).

Jones, A.H.M., *Augustus*, London 1970.

Josephus, *Josephus*, 9 vols. Several translators, Loeb Library 1926–65.

Kennedy, Paul, ed., *Grand Strategies in War and Peace*, New Haven 1991.

Kienast, D., *Augustus: Prinzeps und Monarch*, Darmstadt 1982.

Köberlein, Ernst, *Caligula und die ägyptischen Kulte*, Meisenheim 1962.

Lepelly, C., *Les Cités de l'Afrique romaine*, 2 vols. Paris 1979–81.

Levick, Barbara, *Tiberius the Politician*, London 1976.

Lewis, N., *Life in Roman Egypt*, New York 1983.

Luttwak, Edward N., *The Grand Strategy of the Roman Empire*, Baltimore 1976.

MacKendrick, P., *The Dacian Stones Speak*, North Carolina 1975.

—, *The North African Stones Speak*, North Carolina 1980.

MacMullen, Ramsay, *Enemies of the Roman Order*, Cambridge, Mass. 1967.

Magie, D., *Roman Rule in Asia Minor, to the End of the Third Century after Christ*, Princeton 1950.

Marañón, Gregorio, *Tiberius the Resentful Caesar*, New York 1956.

Marsh, Frank Burr, *The Reign of Tiberius*, Oxford 1931.

Mattingly, Harold, *Coins of the Roman Empire in the British Museum*, London 1976, revised printing of the editions of 1923 and 1965, vol. I: *Augustus to Vitellius*.

Mazzolani, Lidia S., *Tiberio o la spirale del potere*, Milan 1981.

Maurer, Joseph A., *A Commentary on C. Suetonii Tranquilli Vita C. Caligulae Caesaris Chapters I–XXI*, Philadelphia 1949 (University of Pennsylvania dissertation).

Meier, C., *Caesar*, Berlin 1982.

Meise, Eckhard, *Untersuchungen zur Geschichte der Julisch-Claudischen Dynastie*, Munich 1969.

Millar, Fergus, *The Roman Empire and Its Neighbors*, New York 1965.

—, *The Emperor in the Roman World*, London 1977.

Milne, J.G., *History of Egypt under Roman Rule*, London 1924.

Mitchell, S., ed., *Armies and Frontiers in Roman and Byzantine Anatolia*, Oxford 1983.

Mocsy, A., *Pannonia and Upper Moesia*, London 1974.

Mottershead, J., ed., *Claudius/Suetonius*, Bristol 1986.

Nony, Daniel, *Caligula*, Paris 1986.

Ogilvie, R.M., *The Romans and Their Gods in the Age of Augustus*, London and New York 1969.

Passerini, A., *Le coorti pretorie*, Rome, 1939.

Perowne, Stewart, *The Caesars' Wives*, London 1974.

Philo, *Legatio ad Gaium*, trans. E. Mary Smallwood, Leiden 1961.

—, *Philo*, 10 vols. Several translators, Loeb Library 1929–62.

Poulsen, Vagn, *Les portraits romains*, vol. I: *République et dynastie julienne*, Copenhagen 1973.

Quidde, Ludwig, *The Kaiser's Double*, London 1914.

Rager, C.B., *Germania Inferior*, Cologne 1968.

Rajak, Tessa, *Josephus, the Historian and His Society*, London 1983.

Reinhold, Meyer, *Marcus Agrippa*, New York 1933.

—, *History of Purple as a Status Symbol in Antiquity*, Collection Latomus, Vol. 116, Brussels 1970.

Reynold, P.K.B., *The Vigiles of Imperial Rome*, London 1926.

Rhoads, David, *Israel in Revolution, 6–74 C.E.*, Philadelphia 1976.

Roddaz, J.-M., *Marcus Agrippa*, Paris 1984.

Rodewald, Cosmo, *Money in the Age of Tiberius*, Manchester 1976.

Rogers, R.S., *Criminal Trials and Criminal Legislation under Tiberius*, Middletown, Conn. 1935.

Rosborough, Ruskin R., *An Epigraphic Commentary on Suetonius' Life of Gaius Caligula*, Philadelphia 1920 (University of Pennsylvania dissertation).

Sachs, Hanns, *Caligula*, London 1931, trans. Hedvig Singer (originally published in German under the title *Bubi* in 1925).

Scheid, J., *Les frères arvales*, Paris 1975.

Scullard, H.H., *Roman Britain: Outpost of the Empire*, London 1979.

Seager, Robin, *Tiberius*, London and Berkeley 1972.

Seneca, *Moral Essays*, 3 vols, trans. John W. Basore, Loeb Library 1928.

Sitwell, N.H.H., *Roman Roads of Europe*, New York 1981.

Smallwood, E. Mary, *Documents illustrating the Principates of Gaius, Claudius and Nero*, Cambridge 1967.

—, *The Jews Under Roman Rule*, Leiden 1976.

Solinas, PierNico, *Ultimate Porno*, New York 1981.

Solomon, Jon, *The Ancient World in the Cinema*, South Brunswick, N.J. 1978.

Stark, Freya, *Rome on the Euphrates: The Story of a Frontier*, London and New York 1966.

Starr, Chester G., *The Roman Empire 27 BC–AD 476*, New York 1982.

Stevenson, G.H., *Roman Provincial Administration till the Age of the Antonines*, 2nd ed., Oxford 1949.

Suetonius, 2 vols. (trans. John C. Rolfe), Loeb Library 1914.

—, *The Twelve Caesars* (trans. Robert Graves), Harmondsworth 1957.

Sutherland, C.H.V., *The Romans in Spain, 217 BC–AD 117*, London 1939.

Syme, Ronald, *The Roman Revolution*, Oxford 1939.

—, *Tacitus*, 2 vols., Oxford 1958.

—, *History in Ovid*, Oxford 1978.

—, *The Augustan Aristocracy*, Oxford 1986.

Tacitus, *The Complete Works* (trans. A.J. Church and W.J. Brodribb), New York 1942.

—, *The Annals of Imperial Rome* (trans. Michael Grant), Harmondsworth 1971.

Temporini, Hildegard, and Maase, Wolfgang, *Aufstieg und Niedergang der römischen Welt*, a multi-volume, still incomplete publication that began in 1972, Berlin and New York.

Timpe, Dieter, *Der Triumph des Germanicus*, Bonn 1968.

Tuchman, Barbara W., *The March of Folly: from Troy to Vietnam*, New York 1984.

Venturini, Luigi, *Caligola*, 2nd ed., Milan 1906.

Volkmann, Hans, *Cleopatra: A Study in Politics and Propaganda*, London and New York 1958.

Wacher, John, *Roman Britain*, London 1978.

—, *The Roman Empire*, London 1987.

Weingärtner, D.G., *Die Ägyptenreise des Germanicus*, Bonn 1969.

Weinstock, Stefan, *Divus Julius*, Oxford 1971.

Wells, Colin, *The German Policy of Augustus*, Oxford 1972.

—, ed., *Roman Africa: The Vanier Lectures 1980*, Ottowa 1982.

—, *The Roman Empire*, Stanford 1984.
Wiedemann, Thomas, *Adults and Children in the Roman Empire*, New Haven 1989.
Wilken, Robert, *Christians as the Romans Saw Them*, New Haven 1984.
Willrich, Hugo, 'Caligula', *Klio*, 3 (1903), 85–118; 288–317;- 397–470.

—, *Livia*, Leipzig 1911.
Wirszubski, C., *Libertas as a Political Idea at Rome during the Late Republic and Early Principate*, New York 1950.
Yavetz, Z., *Plebs and Princeps*, Oxford 1969.
—, *Julius Caesar and His Public Image*, Ithaca 1983.

Notes

Books are cited in a shortened form (e.g. Starr 1982) and additional bibliographical information may be found in the Select Bibliography. Articles are normally referred to in full in the notes and will not be found in the bibliography. Ancient authors are cited in accordance with commonly used abbreviations. Readers not familiar with those abbreviations will find them resolved in the first few pages of *The Oxford Classical Dictionary*, ed. Hammond and Scullard (1970), a standard reference book available in most libraries. Translations from ancient sources are my own unless stated otherwise.

Preface

1 For the theme in the political philosophy of the Roman Empire generally, see Chester G. Starr, 'Epictetus and the Tyrant', *Classical Philology*, 44 (1949), 20–29. On Caligula specifically, as an example of a bad ruler, see Sen., *De Constantia*, XVIII.
2 Suet., *Calig.*, XXII, 1: 'Hactenus quasi de principe, reliqua ut de monstro narranda sunt.' See my comments in the last chapter on Caligula the 'prince'.
3 The first modern biographer to revise the ancient view of Caligula was the great German historian, H. Willrich, in a series of articles in the journal *Klio*, 3 (1903), 85–118; 288–317; 397–470. He was followed by another well-known German classicist, Matthias Gelzer, who wrote the article on Caligula in the German dictionary of the classical world, *Pauly's Realencyclopädie der klassischen Altertumswissenschaft*, under the title, 'Iulius Caligula', 10 (1918), 381–423. Two biographies in French, by Auguet 1975 and Nony 1986, are in the same tradition. I have not seen the biography by Aalders 1959.

4 See the careful commentaries of Rosborough 1920, Maurer 1949, and Humphrey 1976.
5 Sen., *De Constantia*, XVIII, 4.
6 Barrett 1989, p. 240.
7 Suet., *Calig.*, XXXVI; Dio, LIX, 8, 7.
8 See Barry Baldwin's provocative essay under that title in *Liverpool Classical Monthly*, 9 (1984), 102–5.
9 Suet., *Calig.*, XXX, 2; and Dio, LIX, 30, 1ᶜ. On the deterioration of Caligula's popularity with the people see Yavetz 1969, pp. 116–18.

Chapter One

10 Suet., *Calig.*, VIII, is decisive on this point although some ancient sources do place his birth elsewhere. See Wiedemann 1989, p. 14, for similar problems in the same period. Barrett 1989, pp. 6–7, while not rejecting Suetonius, raises questions.
11 See Weinstock 1971 and Yavetz 1985.
12 For the name Caligula see Suet., *Calig.*, IX, and Dio, LVII, 5, 6.
13 Good, recent surveys of the Roman Empire include Starr 1982, Wells 1984, Garnsey and Saller 1987, and Wacher 1987. See also the pertinent volumes of *The Cambridge Ancient History*. For the Early Empire specifically see Garzetti 1974.
14 Virgil, *Aeneid*, VI, 851–3.
15 Starr 1982, p. 3. On the military frontier see Luttwak 1976 and Ferrill 1986. See also my essay in Kennedy, ed., New Haven 1991, and my book, *Roman Imperial Grand Strategy*, 1991.
16 Stevenson 1949, Hammond 1972 (with an excellent bibliography), and the first chapter of Ennen 1979.
17 For different interpretations of the Augustan constitution see Hammond 1933, Syme 1939, Grenade 1961, Chester Starr, 'How Did Augustus Stop the Roman Revolution?' *Classical Journal*, 52 (1956), 107–12, E.T. Salmon, 'The Evolution of Augustus' Principate', *Historia*, 5 (1956); and Fergus Millar, 'Triumvirate and Principate', *Journal of Roman Studies*, 63 (1973). Also Millar 1977 is fundamental.

18 On this point see Ferrill 1978. See also Wirszubski 1950.

19 Yavetz 1969.

20 Syme 1939, pp. 339 and 371.

21 On Augustus and the aristocracy see Syme 1986.

22 Enid R. Parker, 'The Education of Heirs in the Julio-Claudian Family', *American Journal of Philology*, 67 (1946), 29–50.

23 For good, recent general surveys of the Roman provinces in the Early Empire see Wells 1984 and Wacher 1987. See also P.A. Brunt, 'Charges of Provincial Maladministration Under the Early Principate', *Historia*, 10 (1961), 189–227, and G.P. Burton, 'Proconsuls, Assizes, and the Administration of Justice Under the Empire', *Journal of Roman Studies*, 65 (1975), 92–106.

24 On the publicans in the Late Republic see Badian 1972.

25 Ovid, *Metamorphoses*, I, 175–6.

26 Carettoni 1983. See also Ferdinando Castagnoli, 'Note sulla topografia del Palatino e del Foro Romano', *Archeologia Classica*, 16 (1964), 173–99.

27 Millar 1977, pp. 19–21. See also the interesting discussion by Barrett 1989, pp. 203–10, who argues against a Tiberian date for the *Domus Tiberiana*.

28 Millar 1977, pp. 22–4; Grimal 1984.

29 D'Arms 1970; Millar 1977, pp. 24–8.

30 Augustus, *Res Gestae*, 34, 2, trans. in Braund 1985, p. 21.

31 Bellen 1981; Millar 1977, pp. 61–6.

32 In Caligula's reign there does seem to have been a throne on the Capitol, however, parts of which may still survive. See Barrett 1989, p.203.

33 Reinhold 1970 and Doumet 1980.

34 Wells 1972.

35 Tac., *Ann.*, IV, 5.

36 The best discussion of economy of force in Roman grand strategy is Luttwak 1976, p. 13.

37 Durry 1938 and Passerini 1939.

38 Bellen 1981. See also M. Speidel, 'Germani corporis custodes', *Germania*, 62 (1984), 31–45.

39 Reynold 1926.

40 Freis 1967.

41 See Brent Shaw, 'Fear and Loathing: The Nomad Menace and Roman North Africa', in Wells 1982, pp. 29–50; Lepelly 1979; Fentress 1979.

42 Milne 1924; Lewis 1983.

43 For the eastern frontier see Millar 1965; Colledge 1967; and Stark 1966.

44 The best book is Smallwood 1976, which is heavily documented.

45 Magie 1950.

46 Ferguson 1911.

47 Ferguson 1911.

48 H. Schönberger, 'The Roman Frontier in Germany: An Archaeological Survey', *Journal of Roman Studies*, 59 (1969), 144–97; Broughton 1968; Brogan 1953; Drinkwater 1983; Roger 1968; and Sutherland 1939.

49 Ferrill 1964 has much on Seneca under Caligula, as does Griffin 1976. See also G.W. Clarke, 'Seneca the Younger under Caligula', *Latomus*, 24 (1965), 62–9.

50 See Sitwell 1981, p. 67.

51 Frere 1987; Wacher 1986; Scullard 1979; Dudley and Webster 1965. In the last twenty years many works on Roman Britain have appeared in print.

52 Suet., *Calig.*, XXXII, 3.

53 See the essay by Barbara Levick, 'Julians and Claudians', *Greece & Rome*, 22 (1975), 29–38.

54 Nony 1986, p. 17.

55 On Germanicus see Timpe 1968; Weingärtner 1969; Akveld 1961.

56 Some good books on Caesar and Augustus are Fuller 1965; Gelzer 1968; Meier 1982; Bengtson 1981; Kienast 1982; Grant 1975; Jones 1970; and Earl 1968.

57 On Antony see Carter 1970; Bengtson 1977; and Huzar 1978.

58 On Cleopatra see Grant 1972 and Volkmann 1958.

59 For Livia see Willrich 1911. For her portrait see Brigitte Freyer-Schauenburg, 'Die Kieler Livia', *Bonner Jahrbücher*, 182 (1982), 209–24, and Poulson 1973, who also includes portraits of other figures of the era. For additional portraits of some of the women of the imperial family see L. van Zwet, 'Women's Hair-Dress and the "Grand Camée de France"', *Bulletin van de vereeniging tot bevordering der kennis van de antike beschavig*, 29 (1954), 52–6. The best guide to family relationships in the age of Augustus is Syme 1939 and 1986. See also Meise 1969.

60 On the death of Drusus and on his reputation see Levick 1976, pp. 33–4.

61 On Marcellus see the article in *The Oxford Classical Dictionary*, ed. Hammond and Scullard 1970.

62 There is much on Octavia in Bengtson 1977 and Huzar 1978.

63 On Agrippa see Reinhold 1933 and Roddaz 1984.

64 See Suet., *Tib.*, XXI, whose attempt to disprove the rumours is unconvincing.

65 Arther Ferrill, 'Augustus and His Daughter: A Modern Myth', in Deroux 1980, pp. 332–46. For a different view see Syme 1939, p. 427, and Meise 1969, pp. 5–34. On Julia's mother Scribonia see E. Leon, 'Scribonia and Her Daughters', *Transactions of the American Philological Association*, 82 (1951), 168–75.

66 F.E. Romer, 'Gaius Caesar's Military Diplomacy in the East', *Transactions of the American Philological Association*, 109 (1979), 199–214.

67 On Tiberius in the last years of Augustus see Arther Ferrill, 'Prosopography and the Last Years of Augustus', *Historia*, 20 (1971), 718–31; Levick 1976; and Bogue 1970.

68 Vell. Pat., II, 104, 2.

69 For a recent study of the controversial death of Agrippa Postumus see D. Kehoe, 'Tacitus and Sallustius Crispus', *Classical Journal*, 80 (1985), 247–54. See also Levick 1976, pp. 56–61; 65–7; and 245, n.66.

70 Syme 1978; and Barbara Levick, 'The Fall of Julia the Younger', *Latomus*, 35 (1976), 301–39.

71 Tac., *Ann.*, II, 73.

72 I first emphasized this situation in the article cited above n.67, and was followed by Levick 1976, pp. 47–67.

73 Tac., *Ann.*, I, 53; and Dio, LVII, 18, 1ª.

Chapter Two

74 Suet., *Calig.*, VIII (trans. Robert Graves 1957). See also Parker, n.22, above.

75 Suet., *Calig.*, VIII and Dio, LVI, 26, 1. On Germanicus' commands and honours see Ronald Syme, 'Some Imperial Salutations', *Phoenix*, 33 (1979), 320–25.

76 Suet., *Calig.*, VIII, 5.

77 On this point see V. Massaro and I. Montgomery, 'Gaius – Mad, Bad, Ill, or All Three?', *Latomus*, 37 (1978), 894–909.

78 J.P.V.D. Balsdon, 'Notes Concerning the Principate of Gaius', *Journal of Roman Studies*, 24 (1934), 17.

79 Tac., *Ann.*, I, 31; Vell. Pat., II, 125; Suet., *Tib.*, XXV, 2; Dio, LVII, 5–6.

80 Tac., *Ann.*, I, 31–49. See also Levick 1976, pp. 73–5; Seager 1972, pp. 63–74; Nony 1986, pp. 31–51; and M.A. Giua, 'Germanico nel racconto tacitiano della rivolta delle legioni renane', *Rendiconti dell'Istituto Lombardo*, 110 (1976), 102–13.

81 Seager 1972, pp. 64–5.

82 Tac., *Ann.*, I, 33, mentions hostility between Livia and Agrippina. On the tension between the Julians and Claudians at this time see the items cited above, n.72. On the relations between Tiberius and Germanicus see D.C.A. Shotter, 'Tacitus, Tiberius and Germanicus', *Historia*, 17 (1968), 194–214.

83 The best account of this mutiny is in Tacitus, but see also Suet., *Calig.*, IX; *Tib.*, XXV; and Dio, LVII, 5.

84 Tac., *Ann.*, I, 35.

85 For the Danubian mutiny see Tac., *Ann.*, I, 16–30, Suet., *Tib.*, XXV, Dio, LVII, 4, and Vell. Pat., II, 125.

86 For the letter see Dio, LVII, 5, 3.

87 Tac., *Ann.*, I, 37 (trans. Robert Graves).

88 Tac., *Ann.*, I, 41 (trans. Robert Graves). Dio, LVII, 5, 6, says that troops seized Agrippina and Caligula, then released Agrippina when it became obvious that she was pregnant, but held Caligula briefly. See also Suet., *Calig.*, XLVIII, 1, and Barrett 1989, pp. 9–10, who accepts Dio's version.

89 Tac., *Ann.*, I, 44. See J. Burian, 'Caligula und die Militärrevolte am Rhein', in *Mnema Vladimir Groh* (Prague, 1964), 25–9.

90 Tac., *Ann.*, I, 48.

91 For good portraits of Germanicus and Drusus see V. Poulsen, 'Claudische Prinzen; Studien zur Ikonographie des ersten römischen Kaiserhauses', *Deutsche Beiträge zur Altertumswissenschaft*, 14 (1960), 7–45.

92 T. Mommsen, 'Die Familie des Germanicus', *Hermes*, 13 (1878), 245–65, puts the birth of Agrippina before that of Drusilla, but J. Humphrey, 'The Three Daughters of Agrippina Maior', *American Journal of Ancient History*, 4 (1979), 125–43, argues convincingly that Drusilla was born in February of 15 and Agrippina on 6 November 16. Barrett 1989, pp. 6 and 255, n.7, accepts Mommsen over Humphrey.

93 Dio, LVII, 6, 1 and Tac., *Ann.*, I, 49. See also the discussions in Timpe 1968 and Seager 1972, p. 71.

94 Tac., *Ann.*, I, 49–51.

95 Suet., *Calig.*, IV. For the cancellation of concessions see Tac., *Ann.*, I, 78.

96 B. Gallotta, 'Germanico oltre il Reno', *Acme*, 34 (1981), 293–316.

97 Tac., *Ann.*, I, 55 (trans. Church and Brodribb). See also Timpe 1968; Akveld 1961; Wells 1972; E. Koestermann, 'Die Feldzüge des Germanicus 14–16 n. Chr.', *Historia*, 6 (1957); and J. Ober, 'Tiberius and the Political Testament of Augustus', *Historia*, 31 (1982),

306–28, whose ingenious arguments I cannot accept.

98 Tac., *Ann.*, I, 55–6.

99 Tac., *Ann.*, I, 59.

100 See my *Roman Imperial Grand Strategy* 1991.

101 Tac., *Ann.*, I, 60.

102 Tac., *Ann.*, I, 61–2.

103 Tac., *Ann.*, I, 63–5.

104 Tac., *Ann.*, I, 69 (trans. Church and Brodribb).

105 Tac., *Ann.*, I, 70–72; on the triumph see *Ann.*, I, 55. See also Seager 1972, p. 81.

106 Tac., *Ann.*, II, 5.

107 Tac., *Ann.*, II, 6–8. See also K. Meister, 'Der Bericht des Tacitus über die Landung des Germanicus in der Emsmündung', *Hermes*, 83 (1955), 92–106.

108 Tac., *Ann.*, II, 9–17.

109 Tac., *Ann.*, II, 18–21.

110 Tac., *Ann.*, II, 22.

111 Tac., *Ann.*, II, 23 (trans. Church and Brodribb).

112 Ibid.

113 Tac., *Ann.*, II, 25.

114 Tac., *Ann.*, II, 26.

115 Ibid.

116 Tac., *Ann.*, II, 41 and Vell. Pat., II, 129.

117 Alternatively it may represent Germanicus receiving his commission before departing for the East (Barrett 1989, pp. 12–13). See J.P.V.D. Balsdon, 'Gaius and the Grand Cameo of Paris', *Journal of Roman Studies*, 26 (1936), 152–60, and see also his later note on subsequent discussions in an article, 'The Principates of Tiberius and Gaius', in Temporini, *ANRW*, II, 2, 90. See also H. Jucker, 'Der Grosse Pariser Kameo', *Jahrbuch des Deutschen Archäologischen Instituts*, 91 (1977), 211–50.

118 Tac., *Ann.*, II, 1.

119 Tac., *Ann.*, II, 2–4.

120 Tac., *Ann.*, II, 42.

121 Tac., *Ann.*, II, 43.

122 Tac., *Ann.*, II, 43. See also Levick 1976, pp. 154–7; 96–118; E. Koestermann, 'Die Mission des Germanicus im Orient', *Historia*, 7 (1958), 331–75; Seager 1972, pp. 96–111; and Nony 1986, pp. 71–87. T.T. Rapke, 'Tiberius, Piso, and Germanicus', *Acta Classica*, 25 (1982), 61–9, argues that Piso and Tiberius were not friends and that Livia was responsible for the Governor's appointment. See also D. Sidari, 'La missione di Germanico in Oriente nel racconto di Tacito', *Atti dell'Istituto Veneto di Scienza, Lettere ed Arte*, 138

(1979), 599–628.

123 Tac., *Ann.*, II, 53.

124 Tac., *Ann.*, II, 54. The date was in January or February of 18. See Humphrey in note 92, above.

125 Tac., *Ann.*, II, 55.

126 Tac., *Ann.*, II, 56. On affairs in the East see Braund 1984.

127 Tac., *Ann.*, II, 57.

128 Tac., *Ann.*, II, 58, implies that the insult to Piso was intentional.

129 Weingärtner 1969. See also Levick 1976, pp. 154–5, and D. Hennig, 'Zur Ägyptenreise des Germanicus', *Chiron*, 2 (1972), 349–65.

130 J.H. Oliver, 'On the Edict of Germanicus Declining Divine Acclamations', *Rivista storica dell'Antichità*, 1 (1971), 229–30.

131 Tac., *Ann.*, II, 59–61.

132 Tac., *Ann.*, II, 69.

133 Tac., *Ann.*, II, 71 (trans. Church and Brodribb).

134 Tac., *Ann.*, II, 72 (trans. Church and Brodribb). See Francois D'Erce, 'La mort de Germanicus et les poisons de Caligula', *Janus*, 56 (1969), 123–48. For the date see Barrett 1989, p. 15.

135 Marsh 1931, pp. 69–104 and Wells 1972, pp. 241–5, are especially critical.

136 Tac., *Ann.*, II, 73.

137 Tac., *Ann.*, II, 82.

138 Tac., *Ann.*, III, 1–2.

139 Tac., *Ann.*, III, 6.

140 Tac., *Ann.*, III, 7–10.

Chapter Three

141 On the trial see Rogers 1935; Levick 1976, p. 156; and Seager 1972, pp. 112–18.

142 Tac., *Ann.*, III, 8–9.

143 Tac., *Ann.*, III, 14.

144 Tac., *Ann.*, III, 17.

145 On Sejanus generally see Hennig 1975; R. Sealey, 'The Political Attachments of Aelius Sejanus', *Phoenix*, 25 (1961), 97–114; Z. Stewart, 'Sejanus, Gaetulicus and Seneca', *American Journal of Philology*, 74 (1953), 70–85; H.E. Bird, 'Aelius Sejanus and His Political Significance', *Latomus*, 28 (1969), 61–98; and G.V. Sumner, 'The Family Connections of L. Aelius Sejanus', *Phoenix*, 29 (1965), 134–45.

146 Durry 1938 and Passerini 1939.

147 Tac., *Ann.*, III, 29; Suet., *Claud.*, XXVII, 1; Dio, LVIII, 11, 5.

148 R.S. Rogers, 'Drusus Caesar's Tribunician Power', *American Journal of Philology*, 61 (1940), 457–9. See also K. Scott, 'Drusus,

Nicknamed Castor', *Classical Philology*, 25 (1930), 155–61.

149 Tac., *Ann.*, IV, 2.

150 Tac., *Ann.*, IV, 3 (trans. Church and Brodribb). Levick 1976, p. 161, dismisses the story claiming that Sejanus was acting in self defence and that Livia was not involved. See also Seager 1972, p. 185; and Nony 1986, pp. 127–53.

151 Tac., *Ann.*, IV, 4.

152 Levick 1976, pp. 157–8, cites the evidence.

153 Levick 1976, p. 162.

154 M. Pani, 'Seiano e gli amici di Germanico', *Quaderni di Storia*, 3 (1977), 135–46.

155 Tac., *Ann.*, IV, 15.

156 Tac., *Ann.*, IV, 18–20. They were C. Silius and Titius Sabinus. See D.C.A. Shotter, 'The Trial of Gaius Silius (A.D. 24)', *Latomus*, 26 (1967), 712–16.

157 Tac., *Ann.*, IV, 39–40. See also Seager 1972, pp. 195–9 and Syme 1958, I, 404.

158 Suet., *Tib.*, LII, 1. See also Tac., *Ann.*, IV, 52.

159 See T.P. Wiseman, 'Pulcher Clodius', *Harvard Studies in Classical Philology*, 74 (1970), 207–21.

160 Tac., *Ann.*, IV, 51. See also Seager 1972, p. 201.

161 Levick 1976, pp. 166–7.

162 Tac., *Ann.*, IV, 57 (trans. Church and Brodribb). See also Seager 1972, p. 202.

163 Tac., *Ann.*, IV, 59.

164 Levick 1976, p. 167.

165 There are definite chronological problems for the years after Tiberius' retreat to Capri. See M.P. Charlesworth, 'The Banishment of the Elder Agrippina', *Classical Philology*, 17 (1922), 260–61; R.S. Rogers, 'The Conspiracy of Agrippina', *Transactions of the American Philological Association*, 62 (1931), 160; Meise 1969, p. 240; and Barrett 1989, p. 21.

166 Sen., *De Ira*, III, 21, 5. See also K. Scott, 'Notes on the Destruction of Two Roman Villas', *American Journal of Philology*, 60 (1939), 462.

167 Tac., *Ann.*, IV, 60 (trans. Church and Brodribb).

168 Seager 1972, pp. 206–7.

169 Tac., *Ann.*, IV, 69 (trans. Church and Brodribb).

170 Tac., *Ann.*, V, 3 (trans. Church and Brodribb).

171 Suet., *Tib.*, LIII, LIV, LXIV; *Calig.*, VII.

172 Suet., *Tib.*, LIV, 2; *Calig.*, VII; Dio, LVIII, 3, 8.

173 Seager 1972, p. 213, n.3.

174 Suet., *Tib.*, LXI, 1.

175 Jos., *Antiquities of the Jews*, XVIII, 182; Suet., *Tib.*, LXV, 1; Dio, LXV, 14, 1–2.

176 But see the reservations of John Nicols, 'Antonia and Sejanus', *Historia*, 24 (1975), 48–58.

177 Dio, LVIII, 7, 4.

178 Dio, LVIII, 8, 1–3.

179 Dio, LVIII, 7, 5.

180 Suet., *Tib.*, LIV, 2; LXI, 1; Dio, LVIII, 6, 2–4.

181 Dio, LVIII, 9, 1–2.

182 On Marco see F. de Visscher, 'L'Amphithéâtre d'Alba Fucens et son fondateur Q. Naevius Macro, Préfet du Prétoire de Tibère', *Rendiconti della classe di scienzi morali, storiche e filologiche dell'Academia dei Lincei, Roma*, 12 (1957), 39–49 and 'Macro, préfet des vigiles et ses cohortes contre la tyrannie de Séjan', *Mélanges d'archéologie et d'histoire offerts à A. Piganol* (Paris, 1966), pp. 761–8.

183 Dio, LVIII, 9, 3–6.

184 Dio, LVIII, 10. See also Juvenal, *Satires*, X, 54–80.

185 Tac., *Ann.*, VI, 2 and Suet., *Tib.*, LV, 1.

186 Dio, LVIII, 10.

187 Dio, LVIII, 11, 1–5.

188 Dio, LVIII, 5–7. See Seager 1972, pp. 214–23, and Levick 1976, pp. 173–9. On the whole affair see also A. Boddington, 'Sejanus: Whose Conspiracy?', *American Journal of Philology*, 84 (1963), 1–16.

189 Suet., *Tib.*, LXI, 1.

190 Tac., *Ann.*, VI, 23–4; Suet., *Tib.*, LIV, 2; Dio, LVIII, 22, 4 and 25, 4.

191 Tac., *Ann.*, VI, 25; Suet., *Tib.*, LIII, 2; Dio, 2, 22, 4–5.

Chapter Four

192 Suet., *Calig.*, X; for the date (on which Suetonius is wrong) see Tac. *Ann.*, V, 1.

193 Suet., *Calig.*, LIII. Enid R. Parker, 'The Education of Heirs in the Julio-Claudian Family', *American Journal of Philology*, 67 (1946), 29–50, and Nony 1986, pp. 99–107.

194 For Homer see Suet., *Calig.*, XXII. For oratory see Suet. (cited in note above), and Tac., *Ann.*, XIII, 3. See also F.R.D. Goodyear, 'Tiberius and Gaius: Their Influence and Views on Literature', in Temporini, *ANRW*, II, 32, 1 (1984), 606.

195 At Zaragossa and Carthagena. See Wiedemann 1989, p. 132.

196 Suet., *Calig.*, X.

197 Balsdon 1934, pp. 13–14; Nony 1986, pp. 89–97; and Barrett 1989, p. 24.

198 Balsdon 1934, pp. 117–19, and Barrett 1989, pp. 34–7.
199 Smallwood 1967, no. 401; and Braund 1985, no. 673.
200 Suet., *Calig.*, XXIV.
201 Balsdon 1934, p. 211.
202 Nony 1986, p. 178.
203 Barrett 1989, pp. 25 and 85.
204 Scholiast on Juvenal, IV, 81. See also Barrett 1989, p. 85.
205 Suet., *Calig.*, XII, 1; Dio, LVIII, 8. See also Barrett 1989, p. 260, n.43.
206 Suet., *Calig.*, X, 1.
207 On the making of the *Penthouse* movie see Solinas 1981.
208 Suet., *Tib.*, XLII–XLV.
209 Sachs 1931.
210 Barrett 1989, p. 31.
211 Tac., *Ann.*, VI, 8–9, and Dio, LVIII, 19, 3–5.
212 Wiedemann 1989, p. 117, is probably right in suggesting that Caligula was too old by the time he assumed his toga for a public celebration or ceremony; see also p. 122. Willrich 1903, p. 100, believed that Tiberius did not want Caligula to become conceited. See Barrett 1989, p. 27.
213 There is much conflicting evidence about this marriage. Tac., *Ann.*, VI, 20, 1, dated it to 33. Dio, LVIII, 25, 2, dated it to 35, and Suet., *Calig.*, XII, 1, placed it before Caligula's priesthood in 31. Dio seems the best informed since he is the one who reported the location and the presence of the Emperor; on the other hand, he did not know of the death in childbirth. See Dio, LIX, 8, 7.
214 Tac., *Ann.*, VI, 15.
215 Dio, LX, 27, 4.
216 Barrett 1989, p. 33, somewhat inexplicably, refers to these marriages as 'unimpressive matches'.
217 Suet., *Claud.*, XXXVIII, 3.
218 Tac., *Ann.*, VI, 46.
219 On 'factions' in support of either Caligula or Gemellus see Meise 1969, pp. 50–55.
220 Dio, LVI, 25.
221 Cramer 1954, and MacMullen 1967.
222 Suet., *Aug.*, XCVIII; Dio, LV, 11.
223 Tac., *Ann.*, VI, 45; Suet., *Calig.*, XII, 2; Philo, *Leg. ad Gaium*, XXXIX, 61.
224 Dio, LVIII, 27, 3.
225 Tac., *Ann.*, VI, 46.
226 See the discussions in Balsdon 1964, p. 21, and Barrett 1989, p. 34.
227 Dio, LVIII, 23, 1.
228 Levick 1976, pp. 62–3.

229 Levick 1976, p. 210.
230 Dio, LVIII, 25 (Loeb translation). See also Tac., *Ann.*, V, 10; Levick 1976, p. 292, n.46; and Barrett 1989, p. 33.
231 Tac., *Ann.*, VI, 5 & 9.
232 Philo, *Leg. ad Gaium*, 39 and 61. See also Suet., *Calig.*, XII, 2; Tac., *Ann.*, VI, 45; and Dio, LVIII, 28. Balsdon 1934, pp. 20–21, dismisses the affair as 'unsavoury stories' which he claims have 'little probability'. The tradition is accepted by Nony 1984, pp. 204 and 273, and Barrett 1989, p. 34. It is much too widely attested in ancient authors to be dismissed cavalierly, as it is by Balsdon.
233 Tac., *Ann.*, VI, 20.
234 Tac., *Ann.*, VI, 50; Jos., *Antiquities of the Jews*, XVIII, 224–31; Dio, LVIII, 28; and Suet., *Tib.*, LXXIII.
235 Dio, LIX, 3.
236 Tac., *Ann.*, VI, 46.
237 Suet., *Calig.*, XI.
238 Suet., *Tib.*, LXXVI.
239 Dio, LIX, 1. See Balsdon 1934, pp. 24–9, and Barrett, pp. 50–52.

Chapter Five

240 Suet., *Calig.*, XIII. On Caligula's accession see the comments of P. Grenade, 'Problemes que pose l'avènement de Caligula', *Revue des Études Latines*, 33 (1955), 53–6. See also R. Villers, 'La dévolution du Principat dans la famille d'Auguste', *Revue des Études Latines*, 28 (1950), 235–51; H.M. Cotton, 'Caligula's *Recusatio Imperii*', *Historia*, 34 (1985), 497–503; and the appendix in Barrett 1989, 'The Legal Date of Caligula's Accession', pp. 71–2.
241 Suet., *Calig.*, XIV, 1.
242 Dio, LIX, 3, 1. On the date see Barrett 1989, p. 266, n.28.
243 Dio, LIX, 6, 1.
244 Braund 1985, no. 562.
245 Suet., *Calig.*, XIV, 1 (Loeb translation).
246 For a translation of this famous law see Braund 1985, no. 293. See also P.A. Brunt, 'Lex de Imperio Vespasiani', *Journal of Roman Studies*, 67 (1977), 95–116, and Barrett 1989, pp. 56–7.
247 The most complete is Suet., *Calig.*, L. See also Sen., *De Constantia*, XVIII, 1. and Tac., *Ann.*, XV, 72. For ancient artistic representations of Caligula in sculpture, on coins, and on cameos, see V. Poulsen, 'Portraits of Caligula', *Acta Archaeologica*, 29 (1958), 175–90; Fleming Johansen, 'Antike Porträts von Caligula in der Ny Carlsberg Glyptothek',

Wissenschaftliche Zeitschrift der Humboldt-Universität zu Berlin, 31 (1982), 223–4; Helmut Kyrieleis, 'Zu einem Kameo in Wien', *Archäologischer Anzeiger*, 85 (1970), 492–8; J.C. Faur, 'Un nouveau visage de Caligula', *Acta Archaeologica*, 42 (1971), 35–42; R. Brilliant, 'An Early Imperial Portrait of Caligula', *Acta ad Archaeologiam et Artium Historiam Pertinentia*, 4 (1969), 13–17; Siegfried Laser, 'Zur Ikonographie des Caligula', *Archäologischer Anzeiger* (1954), 241–51; and Poulsen 1973. On the iconography of the age of Caligula generally see Hans Jucker, 'Die Prinzen des Statuenzyklus aus Veleia', *Jahrbuch des deutschen archäologischen Instituts*, 92 (1977), 204–40, and Cesare Salette, 'Tre ritratti imperiali da Luni: Tiberio, Livia, Caligola', *Athenaeum*, n.s. 51 (1973), 34–48.

248 Barrett 1989, p. 43.

249 Suet., *Calig.*, LV, 2. See also D.T. Benediktson, 'Caligula's Madness: Madness of Interictal Temporal Lobe Epilepsy', *Classical World*, 82 (1989), 370–75.

250 Dio, LIX, 3, 8.

251 Dio, LIX, 3, 7.

252 Basildon 1934, pp. 28–9.

253 Dio, LIX, 3, 5.

254 Suet., *Calig.*, XV. On the urns see Balsdon 1934, p. 30.

255 *Corpus Inscriptionum Latinarum*, V, 4953: 'Dis manibus Drusi Caesaris Germ.'

256 Suet., *Calig.*, XV.

257 Suet., *Claud.*, XIV, 1, and Mattingly 1976, I, 154.

258 Suet., *Calig.*, XV and Mattingly 1976, I, cxlvii.

259 Dio, LIX, 3, 4.

260 Suet., *Calig.*, XV.

261 Mattingley 1976, pp. cxlv–cxlvi.

262 Suet., *Claud.*, XI, 2. The Arval records cited by Balsdon (p, 32, n.1) do not refute Suetonius' claim.

263 Suet., *Claud.*, VII, and *Calig.*, XV. See also Dio, LIX, 6, 5–6 and P.A. Gallivan, 'The *Fasti* for the Reign of Gaius', *Antichthon*, 13 (1979), 66–9.

264 On Claudius as an embarrassment see Suet., *Claud.*, IV. Scramuzza, Momigliano and now Levick are among modern scholars who have whitewashed Claudius.

265 Suet., *Calig.*, XV.

266 Ibid.

267 Dio, LIX, 4, 1–3. On the law of treason see J.E. Allison and J.D. Cloud, 'The Lex Julia Maiestatis', *Latomus*, 21 (1962) 711–31.

268 Suet., *Calig.*, XVI and Dio, LIX, 2. See also Balsdon 1934, p. 34.

269 For subsistence income see F.R. Cowell, *Cicero and the Roman Republic*, 104–114. For the cost of housing see Frier 1980.

270 On the games generally see R.F. Newbold, 'The Spectacles as an Issue Between Gaius and the Senate', *Proceedings of the African Classical Association*, 13 (1975), 30–35, and by the same author, 'Cassius Dio and the Games', *L'Antiquité Classique*, 44 (1975), 589–604.

271 Suet., *Calig.*, XIV and Dio, LIX, 3, 2; 6, 1–7.

272 Suet., *Calig.*, XVII and Dio LIX, 7.

273 Suet., *Calig.*, XXIII.

274 Dio, LIX, 3, 6 and Suet., *Calig.*, XXIX. Balsdon 1934 doubts the story, claiming that Antonia's death after one month of Caligula's reign came when the Emperor's conduct was 'still unexceptionable'. Barrett 1989, p. 62, believes that Caligula did not have time to drive Antonia to death, because he was away from the city collecting the remains of his family.

275 Suet., *Calig.*, XIV and Dio, LIX, 8, 1. The main source for his illness is Philo, *Leg. ad Gaium*, 14–23. Balsdon 1934, p. 36, called it a 'nervous breakdown'.

276 See below, n.301.

277 Dio, LIX, 2, 6 and Suet., *Calig.*, XXXVII.

278 See Rodewald 1976 on money under Tiberius.

279 See Keith Hopkins, 'Taxes and Trade in the Roman Empire (200 BC–AD 400)', *Journal of Roman Studies*, 70 (1980), 101–25, and Starr 1982, pp. 86–9.

280 The figure comes from Suetonius. Dio, LIX, 2, 6, gives two slightly different figures, 2,300,000,000 and 3,300,000,000, saying that some sources gave one figure and some the other. Suetonius' figure falls in the middle of the two extremes.

281 Suet., *Nero*, XXX, 1.

282 Suet., *Calig.*, XVI, 1, and Dio, LIX, 9, 4.

283 Suet., *Calig.*, XVI.

284 Ibid.

285 Sen., *Ad Helviam*, X, 4 (Loeb translation).

286 See the items cited above, n.270.

287 Tac., *Hist.*, I, 4, refers to the sordid people (*plebs sordida*) who frequented the theatres and the games. See also Z. Yavetz, 'Plebs Sordida', *Athenaeum*, n.s. 43 (1965), 97ff.

288 On Augustus see Suet., *Aug.*, XLII, 3 and Dio LV, 26, 1; 34, 4. On Tiberius see Suet., *Tib.*, XXXIV, 1; XLVII, Dio LVIII, 1, 1ᵃ, Tac., *Ann.*, IV,

62, and Sen. *De Providentia*, IV, 4.

289 Suet., *Tib.*, XXXVII, 2; Dio, LVII, 21, 3; Tac., *Ann.*, IV, 14, 3.

290 Dio, LIX, 2, 4.

291 Suet., *Calig.*, XXVIII, 3 and Dio, LIX, 5, 2.

292 Suet., *Calig.*, XI.

293 Dio, LXVII, 7, 1.

294 Suet., *Calig.*, XXXVI, 1 and LV, 1; Philo, *Leg. ad Gaium*, 203–5. Dio, LIX, 5, 2, says that Caligula was 'ruled by the charioteers and gladiators, and was the slave of the actors and others connected with the stage. Indeed, he always kept Apelles, the most famous of the tragedians of that day, with him even in public' (Loeb translation).

295 Ibid.

296 Dio, LIX, 7, 5.

297 Dio, LIX, 7, 7.

298 Dio, LIX, 7, 2–3.

299 On the costs see Newbold (cited above, n.270), pp. 32–3.

300 Philo, *Leg. ad Gaium*, 41–51.

301 Philo, *Leg. ad Gaium*, 14–21; Suet., *Calig.*, XIV, 2; and Dio LIX, 8, 1–2. See also V. Massaro and I. Montgomery, 'Gaius – Mad, Bad, Ill or All Three?', *Latomus*, 37 (1978), 894–904, who convincingly argue against the views of Robert S. Katz, 'The Illness of Caligula', *Classical World*, 65 (1972), 223–5, and M. Gwyn Morgan, 'Caligula's Illness Again', *Classical World*, 70 (1977), 451 (who believes Caligula suffered from hyperthyroidism). See also G.C. Moss, 'The Mentality and Personality of the Julio-Claudian Emperors', *Medical History*, 7 (1963), 165–75. A.T. Sandison, 'The Madness of the Emperor Caligula', *Medical History*, 2 (1958), 207, suspects encephalitis.

Chapter Six

302 Suet., *Calig.*, XXVII, 2 and Dio, LIX, 8, 3.

303 René Lugand, 'Suétone et Caligula', *Revue des études anciennes*, 32 (1930), 9–10, attempted to justify these barbarous acts by claiming that gladiatorial combats were part of Roman funeral games and that human sacrifice for the safety of the Emperor was sometimes practised. Even Balsdon 1934, p. 36, n.2, rejected these arguments.

304 Barrett 1989, p. 78.

305 There is simply no evidence for Balsdon's 1934 comment that Caligula's remark was 'probably in jest'. For the story see Suet., *Calig.*, XXIII, 3; Philo, *Leg. ad Gaium*, 62–5; and Dio, LIX, 8, 4–6. There is no evidence that

Silanus was involved in any conspiracy against the Emperor, but see Barrett 1989, pp. 76–7. The voyage referred to here is probably the one the Emperor took to collect the ashes of his family.

306 Suet., *Calig.*, XXIX, 1.

307 Ibid. Philo, *Leg. ad Gaium*, 23–31, gives a slightly different version of his death.

308 See Barrett 1989, p. 75–6, who believes it possible 'that Gemellus was at the centre of an embryonic conspiracy'. Philo, *Leg. ad Gaium*, 23, mentioned that Gemellus was accused of conspiracy but categorically rejected the charge. Otherwise there is no implication of conspiracy at all in ancient authors.

309 Suet., *Calig.*, XXVI, 1 and Dio LIX, 10, 6. See also Philo, *Leg. ad Gaium*, 32–59. For the date see Barrett 1989, p. 78.

310 J. Schwartz, 'Prefets d'Egypte sous Tibère et Caligula', *Zeitschrift für Papyrologie und Epigraphik*, 48 (1982), 189–92.

311 Barrett 1989, p. 78, speculates that Macro conspired with Gemellus and perhaps even Silanus.

312 Philo, *Leg. ad Gaium*, 53–6 (Loeb translation).

313 Bauman 1974, p. 176, thinks it possible that the formal charge was pandering.

314 Balsdon 1934, pp. 38–9. See also Nony 1986, p. 296.

315 Balsdon 1934, p. 40; accepted by Barrett 1989, p. 80.

316 Philo, *Leg. ad Gaium*, 66–73.

317 Suet., *Calig.*, XXV, 1 and Dio, LIX, 8, 7, who says that the marriage lasted two months. Balsdon 1934, pp. 40–41, claimed that Caligula's conduct 'probably evoked little criticism or surprise.' It was only afterwards, 'in a more respectable age', that this marriage was condemned. Barrett 1989, p. 77, says that 'Caligula was, at the very least, excessively impatient.'

318 On this controversial subject see my article, 'The Senatorial Aristocracy in the Early Roman Empire', in Eadie and Ober 1985, pp. 353–71, with full documentation.

319 Suet., *Claud.*, VII–IX.

320 Suet., *Nero*, VI.

321 Suet., *Calig.*, XXIV, 1.

322 Dio, LIX, 22, 6. Balsdon 1934 calls Lepidus the cousin of Caligula and Drusilla, but see L. Hayne, 'The Last of the Aemilii Lepidi', *L'Antiquité classique*, 42 (1973), 497–507. For the family tree, see Barrett 1989, p. 83.

323 Braund 1985, no. 174.

324 Barrett 1989, p. 86, declares that Caligula's behaviour was 'within the bounds of Roman tradition', but no other Roman had ever made his sister a goddess!

325 Suet., *Calig.*, XXIV, 2 (Loeb translation). For the Troy Games in particular see Wiedemann 1989, p. 121.

326 Dio, LIX, 5–6 (Loeb translation). Balsdon 1934, p. 43, dismisses this as 'not so extraordinary after all'.

327 Dio, LIX, 11, 3–4 and Suet., *Calig.*, XXIV, 2.

328 In a much earlier period Romulus was considered to have become a god.

329 Her consecration is confirmed in the records of the Arval Brethren. See Braund 1985, no. 189. See also Peter Herz, 'Die Arvalakten des Jahres 38 n. Chr.', *Bonner Jahrbücher*, 181 (1981), 89–110.

330 See Peter Herz, 'Diva Drusilla', *Historia*, 30 (1981), 324–36. See also Köberlein 1962.

331 There was no official condemnation of Caligula's memory (*damnatio memoriae*), but Claudius did try to disassociate himself from his predecessor. See Edwin S. Ramage, 'Denigration of Predecessor under Claudius, Galba, and Vespasian', *Historia*, 32 (1983), 201–14.

332 Braund 1985, nos. 190, 396 and 673.

333 Barrett 1989, p. 86.

334 Livia was later deified under Claudius. See Suet., *Claud.*, XI, 2.

335 On Lollia Paulina see Suet., *Calig.*, XXV and Dio LIX, 12, 1; 23, 7. On her wealth see Pliny, *Natural History*, IX, 117. As a candidate for marriage with Claudius see Tac., *Ann.*, XII, 1–2; 22. See also James H. Oliver, 'Lollia Paulina, Memmius Regulus and Caligula', *Hesperia*, 25 (1966), 150–53, who argues that Lollia was married to Memmius Regulus according to Greek rather than Roman tradition and that it was less drastic for Caligula to have broken that bond than to have broken a Roman marriage. See also M.B. Flory, 'Caligula's *Inverecundia*: A Note on Dio Cassius 59.12.1', *Hermes*, 114 (1986), 365–71.

336 Suet., *Calig.*, XXV, 2. See also Meise 1966, p. 104, and S. Eitrem, 'Zur Apotheose', *Symbolae Osloense*, 10 (1932), 31–56.

337 Suet., *Calig.*, L, 2.

338 Suet., *Calig.*, XXV.

339 Balsdon 1934, p. 48.

340 For a recent attempt to rationalize this speech see Jean-Claude Faur, 'Un discours de l'empereur Caligula au Sénat (Dion, *Hist. rom.* LIX, 16)', *Klio*, 60 (1978), 439–47, who dates it later in the year in response to the conspiracy of Lepidus and Gaetulicus. He also sees it as a reasonable reassertion of imperial over senatorial rule.

341 Dio, LIX, 16, 3 (Loeb translation). See also Suet., *Calig.*, XXX, 2.

342 Dio, LIX, 16, 4–5 (Loeb translation).

343 Dio, LIX, 16, 11 (Loeb translation).

344 Dio, LIX, 13, 3 (Loeb translation).

345 Dio, LIX, 13, 6. See also Sen., *De Ira*, III, 19, 2.

346 Suet., *Calig.*, XXIII, 1. But Caligula did continue to honour Agrippa on the coins. See John Nicols, 'The Chronology and Significance of the M. Agrippa Asses', *American Numismatic Society: Museum Notes*, 19 (1974), 65–86.

347 Suet., *Calig.*, XXIII, 2.

348 Suet., *Calig.*, XXX, 1

349 Suet., *Calig.*, XXXII, 2.

350 Suet., *Calig.*, XXVII, 4.

351 Ibid.

352 Ibid.

353 Suet., *Calig.*, XXVIII.

354 Suet., *Calig.*, XXXII, 3.

355 Suet., *Calig.*, XXXIII.

356 For the story see Suet., *Calig.*, XIX and Dio, LIX, 17.

357 Suet., *Calig.*, LII.

358 See Barrett 1989, p. 212.

359 Tac., *Hist.*, I, 48.

360 Dio, LIX, 18, 5 (Loeb translation).

361 Suet., *Calig.*, LIII, 2 and Dio, LIX, 19, 7–8. See also J. Stroux, 'Vier Zeugnisse zur römischen Literaturgeschichte der Kaiserzeit', *Philologus*, 86 (1931), 349–55; P. Lambrechts, 'Caligula dictateur littéraire', *Bulletin de l'institut historique belge de Rome*, 28 (1953), 219–30; Jakob Zeyl, 'Seneca's *De Beneficiis* I, 3, 1: *Harena Sine Calce*?', *Classical World*, 72 (1978), 167–71.

362 Dio, LIX, 19, 1–7 (Loeb translation). See also William C. McDermott, 'Saint Jerome and Domitius Afer', *Vigiliae Christianae*, 34 (1980), 19–23.

363 Dio, LIX, 20, 1–2.

364 Balsdon 1934, pp. 207–8 and Petre Ceausescu, 'Caligula et les legs d'Auguste', *Historia*, 22 (1973), 269–83.

Chapter Seven

365 Tac., *Germania*, XXXVII, 5 and *Hist.*, IV, 15, 3.

366 Suet., *Calig.*, XLIII.

367 Barrett 1989, p. 126.

368 On this point see J.P.V.D. Balsdon, 'Notes Concerning the Principate of Gaius', *Journal of Roman Studies*, 24 (1934), 16–17.

Barrett 1989, pp. 104–5, believes that the Emperor went to Lyon rather than to Mainz, and that Gaetulicus was executed before Caligula arrived on the Rhine. But there is no evidence for that view, and Suetonius at least implies that the Emperor went directly to the Rhine.

369 H. Willrich, 'Caligula', *Klio*, 3 (1903), 424, considered this reduction to apply to all imperial troops and praised Caligula for his fiscal policy.

370 Suet., *Calig.*, XLVIII.

371 Tac., *Ann.*, VI, 30.

372 Balsdon 1934, p. 68.

373 See also Dio, LIX, 22, 5, who says that Gaetulicus 'had an excellent reputation in every way', Suet., *Galba*, VI, 3. emphasizes Galba's severity in comparison with Gaetulicus.

374 Z. Stewart, 'Sejanus, Gaetulicus and Seneca', *American Journal of Philology*, 74 (1953), 70–85. See also my 'Seneca's Exile and the *Ad Helviam*: A Reconsideration', *Classical Philology*, 61 (1966), 253–7.

375 Sen., *Ep.* IV, 7. Barrett 1989, p. 107, argues that Lepidus was killed at Mevania in Italy.

376 Suet., *Calig.*, XXIV, 3.

377 Balsdon was certainly wrong in assuming that Domitius Corbulo, 'one of his own friends', replaced one of the two consuls along with Domitius Afer. New archaeological evidence has shown that Corbulo was one of the consuls who was deposed! See P.A. Gallivan, 'The *Fasti* for the Reign of Gaius', *Antichthon*, 13 (1979), 66–9; J. Colin, 'Les consuls du césar-pharaon Caligula et l'héritage de Germani-cus', *Latomus*, 13 (1954), 394–416; and J.W. Humphrey and P.M. Swan, 'Cassius Dio on the Suffect Consuls of AD 39', *Phoenix*, 37 (1983), 324–7. Balsdon took no note of this in his later review of scholarship on the period, 'The Principates of Tiberius and Gaius', in Temporini, *ANRW*, II, 2, 86–94.

378 Balsdon's reconstruction, however, has been widely accepted. See Peter Bicknell, 'The Emperor Gaius' Military Activities in AD 40', *Historia*, 17 (1968), 498. For views before 1934 see Balsdon 1934, Appendix A, pp. 220–21.

379 Suet., *Calig.*, LIX.

380 On the political implications of the marriage with Caesonia see Barrett 1989, p. 110.

381 Virgil, *Aeneid*, I, 207.

382 Suet., *Calig.*, XLV.

383 Dio, LIX, 22, 2. See R. Syme, 'Some Imperial Salutations', *Phoenix*, 33 (1979), 325.

384 For the order see Dio, LIX, 22, 9.

385 Suet., *Claud.*, IX, 1 and Dio, LIX, 23, 2–5.

386 Suet., *Calig.*, XXXIX, 1 and Dio, LIX, 21.

387 Suet., *Calig.*, XXXIX, 2.

388 Dio, LIX, 22, 4.

389 Dio, LIX, 24, 6 (Loeb translation).

390 Dio, LIX, 24, 6–8.

391 Suet., *Calig.*, XX.

392 Juvenal, *Satires*, I, 41–4 (trans. Hubert Creekmore, *The Satires of Juvenal*, New York 1963, p. 27).

393 Suet., *Galba*, V, 2–3.

394 See my comments in *Roman Imperial Grand Strategy*, 1991. Barrett 1989, pp. 126–9, argues that hostile Britons threatened Gaul, but that seems unlikely.

395 Dio, LIX, 25, 5ᵃ. Barrett 1989, p. 138, believes that Caligula was only jokingly given the name Britannicus, but that is certainly not true of the name Germanicus, which is referred to in the same sentence.

396 Suet., *Calig.*, XLIV, 2. On Amminus see M. Henig and D. Nash, 'Amminus and the Kingdom of Verica', *OJA*, 1 (1982), 243–6.

397 For recent modern attempts to rationalize it see R.W. Davies, 'The "Abortive Invasion" of Britain by Gaius', *Historia*, 15 (1966), 124–8; Peter Bicknell, 'The Emperor Gaius' Military Activities in AD 40', *Historia*, 17 (1968), 496–505; and E.J. Phillips, 'The ·Emperor Gaius' Abortive Invasion of Britain', *Historia*, 19 (1970), 369–74. See also Balsdon 1934, pp. 88–93.

398 The arguments of Peter Bicknell (see note above) in favour of Lower Germany and the North Sea rather than Gaul and the English Channel are not convincing.

399 Suet., *Calig.*, XLVI and Dio, LIX, 25, 2–4. See also Tac., *Agricola*, XIII, 4. Suetonius said that Caligula built the lighthouse afterwards, but that is probably an error. On the tower see F. d'Erce, 'La tour de Caligula à Boulogne-Sur-Mer', *Revue Archéologique* (1966), 89–96, though his defence of the wisdom of Caligula cannot be supported by the tower itself.

400 Suet., *Calig.*, XLVII.

401 Suet., *Calig.*, XLVIII.

402 Balsdon 1934, p. 92.

403 See P.J. Bicknell, 'Gaius and the Sea-Shells', *Acta Classica*, 5 (1962), 72–4, who effectively dismisses Balsdon's arguments: 'First, "*musculi*" were not the most prominent of the siege engines, and it is hardly likely that "embark the sappers' huts" was one of the major, or the more memorable, of the orders given on this particular occasion' (p. 73).

However, Bicknell's explanation was as far-fetched as Balsdon's, and he retracted it in a later article, calling it 'rather fanciful'. See Bicknell's article, p. 500, cited above, n.397.

Chapter Eight

404 Dio, LIX, 23, 9.
405 Sen., *De Ira*, III, 19, 2.
406 Suet., *Calig.*, XLVIII,2–XLIX,1–2.
407 Suet., *Calig.*, XLIX, 3.
408 Dio, LIX, 20, 5.
409 Dio, LIX, 25, 5. For the statistics from the chronographer of the year 354 see Balsdon 1934, p. 97.
410 Suet., *Calig.*, XXIX (Loeb translation).
411 See the discussion by I.E. Grady, 'Dio LIX. 25. 5ᵇ, A Note', *Rheinisches Museum für Philologie*, 124 (1981), 261–7, which supersedes Balsdon 1934, p. 99. In addition to the passage in Dio, see Sen., *De Ira*, III, 18, 3–4.
412 Suet., *Calig.*, XXXII.
413 Suet., *Calig.*, XXIII.
414 Suet., *Calig.*, LII.
415 Suet., *Calig.*, LIV.
416 Suet., *Calig.*, XXXVII.
417 Suet., *Calig.*, XXXVII, 2.
418 There is a good discussion of these ships in Barrett 1989, pp. 201–2.
419 Sen., *Ep.*, XXIX, and *De Beneficiis*, II, 21, 5.
420 Tac., *Agricola*, IV, 1.
421 Sen., *De Ira*, II, 3–4.
422 Dio, LIX , 26, 1–2.
423 Dio, LIX, 26, 3.
424 Barrett 1989, p. 159.
425 Dio, LIX, 26, 5 (Loeb translation). See also the many comments on this matter in Philo, *Leg. ad Gaium*.
426 Philo, *Leg. ad Gaium*, 78 and 93.
427 Suet., *Calig.*, XXII and Dio LIX, 26, 5–10. See also M.P. Charlesworth, '"Deus Noster Caesar"', *Classical Review*, 39 (1925), 114.
428 Dio, LIX, 26, 8–9 (Loeb translation).
429 Dio, LIX, 27, 5–6.
430 Sen., *De Beneficiis*, II, 12 (Loeb translation). See also Jos., *Antiquities of the Jews*, XIX, 32–6; Suet., *Calig.*, XVI, 4; and Dio, LIX, 26, 4.
431 Sen., *De Ira*, I, 8–9 (Loeb translation). See also Marta Giacchero, 'Le reminiscenze erodotee in Seneca e la condanna di Caligola', *Sandalion*, 3 (1980), 175–89.
432 Suet., *Calig.*, XXII, 2; LVII, 1 and Dio, LIX, 28, 3. See also Jos., *Antiquities of the Jews*, XIX, 8–10. The cautionary comments of C.J. Simpson, 'The Cult of the Emperor Gaius',

Latomus, 40 (1981), 489–511, that the association of Caligula and Jupiter was based on rivalry, rather than identification, with the god, and that Caligula was not formally deified, deserve careful reading. I personally believe that the literary evidence, that Caligula considered himself to be a god and required others to treat him as one, is overwhelming. Since the cult could not have lasted more than a few months, from the summer of 40 to the Emperor's death in January of 41, there are otherwise few traces of it.

433 Dio, LIX, 28, 5–6 and Suet., *Calig.*, XXII, 2.
434 Suet., *Calig.*, XXII, 3 (Loeb translation).
435 Dio. LIX, 28, 1, and Suet., *Calig.*, XXI.
436 Braund 1985, no. 181.
437 Balsdon 1934, p. 165.
438 Barrett 1989, p. 151.
439 Tac., *Ann.*, IV, 37–8.
440 Balsdon 1934, pp. 165–6.
441 Suet., *Calig.*, XXII, 1. See also Alessandro Aiardi, 'Optimus Maximus Caesar: considerazioni sull'interesse di Caligola per il culto di Giove', *Atti dell'Istituto Veneto di Scienze, Lettere ed Arti*, 136 (1977–8), 99–108.
442 Braund 1985, no. 558 B.
443 Balsdon 1934, p. 169.
444 Two good books on the subject are Ogilvie 1969 and Wilken 1984.
445 Barrett 1989, p. 153.

Chapter Nine

446 The basic study of the Jews under the Romans is Smallwood 1976, but recently there has been a spate of books. See Rhoads 1976, Rajak 1983, Goodman 1987, Applebaum 1989, and Feldman and Hata 1987 and 1989.
447 Tac., *Hist.*, V, 9 (trans. Church and Brodribb). See also P.W. Barnett, '"Under Tiberius All Was Quiet"', *New Testament Studies*, 21 (1975), 564–71.
448 Pontius Pilate was *Praefectus Iudaeae* (not Procurator), as is revealed in an inscription discovered in 1961. For the inscription see Braund 1985, no. 437. See also Smallwood 1976, pp. 145 and 167, n.79.
449 Paul L. Maier, 'The Fate of Pontius Pilate', *Hermes*, 99 (1971), 362–71, argues '. . . that Pilate, while hardly a master of diplomacy, was at least trying to make the best of very difficult administrative situations.'
450 S.J. De Laet, 'Le successeur de Ponce Pilate', *L'Antiquité Classique* (1939), 418–19, discusses the implications of replacing Pontius

Pilate, though his conclusion has not received wide acceptance.

451 Luke 13.32.

452 The date is controversial. Barrett 1989, p. 229, n.8, places it in the year 40.

453 On the place of banishment see Jos., *Antiquities of the Jews*, 18, 252, and the comments of Barrett 1989, p. 299, n.10.

454 H.I. Bell, 'Antisemitism in Alexandria', *Journal of Roman Studies*, 31 (1941), 1–18.

455 On the Jewish courts see Goodenough 1968.

456 Jewish quarters in the city were not exactly a ghetto. See Smallwood 1976, p. 225: 'But these districts did not form a ghetto. The geographical concentration of alien groups is a regular feature of large cities, and the Jews were granted a special quarter as a privilege, not confined to it as a disability.'

457 Smallwood 1976, p. 240.

458 On the problem of chronology see Barrett 1989, p. 300, n.22.

459 On the differences between Philo's and Josephus' accounts of this story see E. Mary Smallwood, 'Philo and Josephus as Historians of the Same Event', in Feldman and Hata 1987, pp. 114–29.

460 P. Fraccaro, 'C. Herennius Capito di Teate, procurato di Livia, di Tiberio e di Gaio', *Athenaeum*, 28 (1940), 141–4, and H. Fuhrmann, 'C. Herennius Capito', *Epigraphica*, 2 (1940), 25–9.

461 E.M. Smallwood, 'The Chronology of Gaius' Attempt to Desecrate the Temple', *Latomus*, 16 (1957), 3–17. But the problem is complicated; see also P. Bilde, 'The Roman Emperor Gaius (Caligula)'s Attempt to Erect His Statue in the Temple of Jerusalem', *Scandinavian Journal of Theology*, 32 (1978), 67–93.

462 Philo, *Leg. ad Gaium*, 266–75.

463 S. Zeitlin, 'Did Agrippa Write a Letter to Gaius?', *JQR*, 56 (1965–6), 22–31, challenges the authenticity of the letter but has not been followed by most scholars.

464 According to another version, Petronius angered Caligula by refusing to withdraw his troops from Ptolemais, and the Emperor ordered him to commit suicide, but the order arrived after Caligula had died. See P. Winter, 'Simeon der Gerechte und Caius Caligula', *Judaica*, 12 (1956), 129–32.

Chapter Ten

465 Barrett 1989, p. xix.

466 D. Fishwick and B.D. Shaw, 'The Formation of Africa Proconsularis', *Hermes*, 105 (1977), 369–80.

467 Tac., *Ann.*, IV, 23–6.

468 For the date see Barrett 1989, p. 117. See also D. Fishwick, 'The Annexation of Mauretania', *Historia*, 20 (1970), 470.

469 Dio, LIX, 25, 1, and Suet., *Calig.*, XXXV, 1. See also Sen., *De Tranquillitate*, XI, 12. On the purple cloak see M. Hoffman, 'Ptolemais von Mauretania', cited in Barrett 1989, pp. 117–18, and p. 284, n.12.

470 D. Fishwick and B. Shaw, 'Ptolemy of Mauretania and the Conspiracy of Gaetulicus', *Historia*, 25 (1976), 491–4. See also J.C. Faur, 'Caligula et Mauretanie: La Fin de Ptolémée', *Klio*, 55 (1973), 249–71, and T. Kotula, 'Encore sur la mort de Ptolémée de Maurétanie', *Archaeologia*, 15 (1964), 76–94.

471 Barrett 1989, p. 119.

472 Tac., *Hist.*, IV, IV, 48, and Dio, LIX, 20, 7.

473 Barrett 1989, p. 120.

474 On Caligula's drinking see Jerome 1923, pp. 419–21.

475 Luttwak 1976, pp. 30–40. On the client kings generally see Braund 1984.

476 Ferrill 1991.

477 See my article, 'Rome's Mistake in Britain', forthcoming in 1991 in *MHQ: The Quarterly Journal of Military History*.

478 Suet., *Calig.*, XIV, 14, 3; Dio, LIX, 27, 3; and Jos., *Antiquities of the Jews*, XVIII, 102.

479 Tac., *Ann.*, XI, 8, 1; Dio, LX, 8, 1; and Sen., *De Tranquillitate*, XI, 12.

480 Tac., *Ann.*, XI, 8–9, and Dio, LX, 8, 1.

481 Willrich 1903, p. 301. Not even Balsdon 1934, p. 199, and Barrett 1989, p. 64, go that far.

482 See J. Sullivan, 'Thrace in the Eastern Dynastic Network', in Temporini 1979, II, 7, 1, pp. 207–11. See also A. Barrett, 'Polemo II of Pontus and M. Antonius Polemo', *Historia*, 27 (1978), 437, for the date.

483 Dio, LIX, 12, 2.

484 Barrett 1989, p. 222.

485 Dio, LIX, 8, 2 and 24, 1.

486 Suet., *Calig.*, XVI, 3.

Chapter Eleven

487 Suet., *Calig.*, XXII, 1.

488 That is surely the meaning of Dio, LX, 6, 8–9. Suet., *Calig.*, XXI, states categorically that Caligula rebuilt the theatre. Barrett 1989, p. 303, n.21, believes that Balsdon made a mistake on this point, but close reading of Dio confirms Balsdon's view. See Balsdon 1934, p. 175. See also Suet., *Tib.*, XLVII and Tac., *Ann.*, III, 72, 2.

489 Suet., *Calig.*, XXXV, 1, and Dio, LX, 5, 9; 31, 7.

490 Barrett 1989, p. 49.

491 Suet., *Calig.*, XXXVI.

492 Suet., *Calig.*, LV, 2.

493 Suet., *Calig.*, I, 2.

494 Dio, LIX, 14, 1–4.

495 Suet., *Calig.*, XXXVIII, 4.

496 Dio, LIX, 14, 6. See also Suet., *Calig.*, LIV, 1.

497 See Barrett 1989, pp. 196–201, for a thorough discussion.

498 Dio, LIX, 14, 5.

499 Suet., *Calig.*, LV, 2.

500 Suet., *Calig.*, LV, 3, and Dio, LIX, 14, 7.

501 Suet., *Calig.*, XVIII, 3.

502 Suet., *Calig.*, LVIII, 1, gives this date, but there is some uncertainty. Nevertheless the assassination, if it was not on the day Suetonius says, was within a few days of 24 January. See Barrett 1989, pp. 169–71.

503 Tac., *Ann.*, XI, 29, 1.

504 Suet., *Calig.*, LVI, 1.

505 Jos., *Antiquities of the Jews*, XIX, 45.

506 Sen., *De Constantia*, XVIII, 3. See also Suet., *Calig.*, LVI, 2; Dio, LIX, 29, 2; and Jos., *Antiquities of the Jews*, XIX, 20–21.

507 Suet., *Calig.*, LVIII, 2; Dio, LIX, 29, 1; and Jos., *Antiquities of the Jews*, XIX, 46.

508 Tac., *Ann.*, VI, 9, 5–7; Dio, LX, 15, 1; and Jos., *Antiquities of the Jews*, XIX, 20.

509 Sen., *De Constantia*, XVIII, 2.

510 Jos., *Antiquities of the Jews*, XIX, 159, and Tac., *Ann.*, XI, 1–3.

511 Some modern scholars believe that Rufus was the main source of Josephus, Suetonius, and Dio Cassius. See Balsdon 1934, pp. 222–8, but there are problems with the identification. See Barrett 1989, pp. 168–9.

512 Jos., *Antiquities of the Jews*, XIX, 123.

513 Suet., *Calig.*, LVIII, 1. See the appendix in Barrett 1989, pp. 169–71, 'The Date and Location of Caligula's Death.'

514 Jos., *Antiquities of the Jews*, XIX, 80–83, and Philo, *Leg. ad Gaium*, 250 and 338.

515 Suet., *Calig.*, LVII.

516 Suet., *Calig.*, LVII, 4; Jos., *Antiquities of the Jews*, XIX, 87.

517 Dio, LIX, 29, 5.

518 Suet., *Calig.*, LVI, 2, and LVIII, 1; and Jos., *Antiquities of the Jews*, XIX, 96–103.

519 Suet., *Calig.*, LVII, 1; Jos., *Antiquities of the Jews*, XIX, 102–5; and Dio, LIX, 29.

520 Suet., *Calig.*, LVIII, 2–3.

521 Suet., *Calig.*, LVIII, 3; Dio, LIX, 29, 7; and Jos., *Antiquities of the Jews*, XIX, 105–13.

522 Jos., *Antiquities of the Jews*, XIX, 153–6.

523 Suet., *Calig.*, LVIII, 3; Dio, LIX, 59, 30b; and Jos., *Antiquities of the Jews*, XIX, 123–6.

524 Suet., *Calig.*, LX.

525 Suet., *Calig.*, LV, 3 and Dio, LIX, 14, 7.

526 Suet., *Calig.*, LIX, and Jos., *Antiquities of the Jews*, XIX, 190–200. See also Barrett 1989, pp. 166–7.

527 Dio LIX, 30 (Loeb translation).

Epilogue

528 Dio, LIX, 24, 1, who refers specifically to Agrippa and Antiochus.

529 Suet., *Calig.*, LXIX, and Jos., *Antiquities of the Jews*, XIX, 237.

Illustration Acknowledgments

Numbers refer to pages

Florence: Archaeological Museum 67 l (Photo German Archaeological Institute, Rome); London: British Museum 66 l, 68 t, 69 t, 70 tr, 70 tl, 70 b, 71 t, 71 b; Paris: Musée du Louvre 65 (Photo Réunion des Musées Nationaux), Bibliothèque Nationale 72 (Photo Giraudon); Ravenna: Museo di S. Vitale 66 br; Rome: Museo Nationale delle Terme 66 t (Photo Alinari/Anderson), Capitoline Museum 67 r (Photo Alinari/Anderson); Roman villa at Nennig 68 bl, 68 br, 69 b (Photo Staatliche Bildstelle, Saarbrücken); map by The Graphic Line (Robert Thorn) 22–3; drawing by Ian Mackenzie-Kerr 5

Index

Page numbers in italic refer to illustrations

Index